THE SPEED OF GRACE

THE SPEED OF GRACE

Jason Mayden

"I know if I'm generous at heart,
I don't need recognition.
The way I'm rewarded—well,
that's God's decision."

—KENDRICK LAMAR

TRILLICON®

TRILLICON VALLEY®

THE SPEED OF GRACE

ISBN

979-8-88926-000-4 *Paperback*

979-8-88926-002-8 *Hardcover*

979-8-88926-001-1 *eBook*

To my family and loved ones near and far, may you find peace as you surrender your burdens and abandon your worry.

What is meant for you will find you when you are ready. Open your heart to the magic and wonder of the moment. Abandon your hesitation and despair. May your heart sing a song of praise and may your soul find respite. We need you to shine bright as you do everything with honor and gratitude. Rise above your circumstances, beloved. You are fearfully and wonderfully made. God provides.

—Jason Mayden, November 2, 2022

CONTENTS

AUTHOR'S NOTE

The road I took to avoid my destiny led me right back to it.

South Side of Chicago
October 12, 2019, 7:14 a.m.

On a brisk autumn morning, I sat outside my childhood home, staring at the facade of a place I once occupied. Immense bewilderment overtook me while I studied the details of what remained. Wild ivy had reclaimed the weathered redbrick exterior. Nature's silent wrath engulfed my vivid memories of bullying and disparagement.

A sense of order and refinement in the neatly manicured lawn sat juxtaposed against a backdrop of decay. A flatbed truck was parked near the curb. I imagined it symbolically carrying away the pain of my former low self-worth to make space for the joy and abundance of my present reality.

At 8:12 a.m., I arrived at Foot Locker, the place that had served as a refuge of peace in my teenage years. The sun danced across the parking lot, playfully glistening on the surfaces of the cars of the employees who had come to hear me speak about my journey from south-side kid to founder, CEO, world-renowned lecturer, and award-winning designer. It was all too surreal. None of this was supposed to happen for a shy, neurodivergent kid who struggled to find belonging among his peers.

The small group of guests filled the Foot Locker sales floor with energetic conversations and warm salutations. The diverse group of attendees, who typically only gathered in mass for moments of remembrance or mourning, had formed a tribe focused on love and community. They had found a sense of calm in each other's presence.

For the next hour, I passionately discussed how twenty-five years ago, I stared out the windows of that store with a heart full of angst, wondering when it would be the right moment to find a safe passage on my way home.

As the attentive audience of police officers, community activists, street evangelists, and sneaker enthusiasts surrounded me, I knew my story had the power to transcend the invisible socio-economic, race, and class boundaries. We were all of one tribe, standing together to find a way to inspire and care for our youth.

I had a chance to motivate them through my words, lived experience, and philosophy.

As an adult, creativity had become my "jump shot." It had afforded me a life I could never have imagined. Yet, in my heart, I knew the time had come for me to serve as an example for the countless creative youths whose peers often reject or misunderstand.

The most important lessons I shared that day have continued to be some of the most relevant topics I speak about around the world:

Creative entrepreneurship will radically overhaul the opportunity landscape for marginalized youth. Authentically pursuing your interests—not those your ethnicity, gender, location of birth, or other demographics assign—can help you find or create a place of acceptance and adoration within an industry.

Intergenerational trauma is an immense burden. Pain as a source of inspiration has diminishing returns. Therapy as a mechanism of healing is a radical act of self-love. Mental restitution should be a fundamental human right.

When gracefully exploring the maturation of creativity as a form of rebellion against the status quo, and when opportunity meets preparation, miraculous things can and do happen.

The Speed of Grace is not intended to be a perfect book. Instead, this collection of deeply personal reflections guides the reader through the behaviors and principles I used to pursue creative, physical, professional, personal, and emotional growth.

My mission is simple. Through vulnerability, transparency, and authenticity, I seek to inspire *you*, the reader, to conquer the fears and insecurities you have yet to confront, to heal from the wounds of the past that block your blessings in present reality, and to view creativity as a form of altruistic rebellion.

Historically marginalized creatives must now lead movements, identify new opportunities for collective healing, and influence organizations and communities at all levels. Designing beautiful products, services, and experiences is no longer enough.

This newfound focus on adopting the designer's mindset in business and society has placed creatives in a profound position of privilege and responsibility, but are we ready to step up and lead?

Have we been given good examples and instructions for healing from our intergenerational trauma? Are we being taught how to assess personal and professional developmental gaps through empathy and introspection, or are we creating conditions that could lead to burnout and creative fatigue?

Throughout my twenty-plus-year career as an award-winning designer, lecturer, entrepreneur, and academic, I have learned the power of addressing my inner pain. As a result, I successfully healed the hurt of personal and professional disappointment and unleashed my creativity through the filters of immersive empathy, introspective curiosity, and emotional neutrality.

In this moment, the power and potential of creativity in marginalized communities is helping to break the binds of economic disparagement, toxic environments, food insecurity, and destructive narratives.

We are learning.

We are healing.

We are rising.

We are the ones we have been waiting for.

Our time is now.

#WAGMI

CHAPTER 1

THE FALLACY OF FEAR

"Death and life are in the power of the tongue [. . .]." Proverbs 18:21 NKJV

Growing up in a Baptist family on the south side of Chicago, I was consistently confronted with this reference to Proverbs 18:21. I understood the words I spoke to myself and others could be used to build or destroy. As a result, I choose my words carefully when expressing thoughts, perspectives, and anecdotes. I seek to speak life over my circumstances. I prefer to use words as a way to heal rather than to disrupt. While this way of existing works well in my personal life, I often have been severely disappointed when applying this precept in professional settings.

In those who entrust us to lead, words, tone, and projected energy all contribute to the presence of peace or the lingering sting of belittlement, which brings about inward eruptions of despair resulting from managerial insensitivity. Poor managers' degrading behavior is intended to break the wills of neophytes and veterans alike.

Disruptive leaders in corporate America commonly desire authority rather than accountability in most organizational structures. Unfortunately, their misguided ethos provides a sense of unbridled power, and they often ridicule the empathetic leaders who gain trust through humility and self-awareness.

Through coercion and subjugation, they aim to control the output and self-efficacy of newly hired creatives.

This "leadership by force" type has become the norm in modern creative organizations. Creative influencers' emotionally charged, erratic behavior is heralded as a brave form of leadership.

Unfortunately, this toxic form of power wielded in the social media age leads young and seasoned creatives down a dangerous path. If left unchecked, we ultimately could become like the people who have long misunderstood the value of our nuanced perspectives. We become the "they" in every complaint.

"They don't want us to win."

"They don't care about us."

"They want to use the culture for personal gain."

I am sure you have heard some of these statements or even said something similar.

Throughout my professional journey, I have encountered my fair share of self-absorbed leaders. They can be easily spotted in every professional setting by how they leverage their position of authority to mercilessly shroud their lack of intelligence, preparation, or attention to detail. They exude false confidence and passionately deflect when held accountable to the standards of their professional context. I have never been in harmony with these types of people. My natural desire to build genuine relationships exposes me to being disappointed when my intentions are misinterpreted.

Introspection can be highly uncomfortable for leaders who do not have the professional maturity to carry the weight and responsibility of their title.

Looking back, I now have a clearer picture of where my aversion to this style of leadership began. As a seven-year-old child navigating the psychological and emotional microaggressions of a system designed to dismantle my identity, I was often overwhelmed with confusion when my teachers called out and ridiculed my behavior.

I remember when I first felt attacked by the prejudice of a culturally ignorant educator. At seven years old, I surpassed the national aptitude and intelligence standard. I was beyond measurement and analysis. I was Black, energetic, and creative. As a result, my teacher assumed I had ADHD at the time due to my constant movement in the classroom. Years later, at thirty-eight, I discovered I actually was neurodivergent and had a form of high-functioning autism called Asperger's syndrome.

The term "neurodivergent" refers to the idea that differences in the human brain are natural and normal and, in many cases, can lead to meaningful and positive insights and abilities. People are described as neurodiverse when their thought patterns, behaviors, or learning styles fall outside what is considered "normal" or neurotypical (Rudy 2022).

Consequently, I felt as if my second-grade teacher treated me like I was "broken." I was a highly cerebral boy from a lower middle-class home, and she could not fathom that my different thinking style was a form of creative intelligence. She wanted someone to label and dismiss. God wanted someone to use and uplift.

She would patrol the classroom looking for the right moment to pounce on any behavior she deemed "disruptive" to the overall learning environment. She would study and deeply critique my physical movement, which usually increased as I sat, bored, waiting on the next classroom activity to begin.

Despite showing signs of tremendous creativity and intellectual curiosity, my teacher decidedly ignored my potential. Rather than finding joy in nurturing a child's budding imagination, she criminalized my behavior.

It wasn't long before I discovered the depths of her desire to break my spirit. My teacher made it a point to openly critique everything about me, ritualistically embarrassing me daily in the classroom.

"What's wrong with your hair?"

"My gosh, why are you so messy?"

"Oh, you think you are smarter than me, huh?"

My hair texture, clothes, and even the fact that I was academically gifted would become the basis of her persistent attacks. Her remarks pushed me toward anger and hurt. I would retreat into my imagination as a way to disassociate my inner dialogue from my present reality. Instead, I would pour my pain into my art, which ultimately proved to be both a blessing and a burden.

In the fall of 1987, I reached a shattering point. Her constant critiques, sharp and precise, pierced my heart and confidence, rupturing my sense of worth and desire to be a "good" student.

In my seven-year-old mind, I rationalized that if a person could mistreat me without any regard for my well-being, I was entitled to express myself through my art as a form of rebellion. So I sat, pulled my pencil case from my desk, and created what would become the catalyst for my entire artistic career.

Each line was like a lash intended to express my anger and dissatisfaction with her dismissive labeling. But instead, the imagery reinforced my aspirations, and the words captured my youthful, rebellious spirit. I spent the next few minutes finalizing a drawing of a young boy standing proudly on a pedestal, poised with a wide grin. Across his chest was a rocket that had just taken flight, evident by the round smoke clouds directly below the exhaust pipe.

While this image was innocent as an independent element of the drawing, it had become the center point of my teacher's controversial interpretation of the subject matter. To make things worse, I had drawn the character with a middle finger raised and a prominent speech bubble above the head with the words "f——k you" written with the proficiency of a seven-year-old child.

This was a direct response to her false critiques. I thought my creation was imaginative, but my teacher begged to differ.

"Oh my gosh, what is this?" Her voice startled me. I had no clue she was standing behind me while I added the finishing touches to the now-infamous sketch. Surprisingly, she appeared both offended *and* impressed.

The quality of the drawing must have shown the early indicators of my talent while the subject matter revealed my intelligence and situational comprehension. Nevertheless, my teacher immediately scolded me, and I was told a letter would be sent home to my parents.

"Ooh. You in trouble," the class collectively exclaimed as I sat staring at my desk in embarrassment.

I was in trouble, and there was no way out of it.

I carried the letter home in my backpack with the nerves of a person tasked with holding a ticking time bomb. I knew my parents would be livid. Several weeks earlier, my teacher urged them to put me on Ritalin as a form of behavioral modification.

As expected, my parents vehemently opposed this blanket diagnosis and the recommendation of drug-induced stillness. Instead, they advocated for me to be allowed to draw in class to occupy my mind.

I was undeniably intelligent, and my work was completed on time, accurately, and with great detail. However, as a neurodivergent child, I would fidget—a lot. My parents were used to being notified by letter of my classroom progress. However, this time was different. My teacher had also requested to speak with them.

Upon returning home, I slowly walked into the kitchen and sheepishly handed the letter to my mom, who was standing, phone in hand, cord dangling, with a look of frustration. She'd had enough. As I braced for my impending punishment, something shifted. My mother, while speaking with my teacher, fought back laughter.

"Hi, Mrs. V. Thank you for the letter and the call. Jason has a vivid imagination. I'm sure that is indeed a rocket." She signaled with a hand gesture for me to stay silent as she spoke with my teacher. I was utterly shocked, watching her discuss the drawing with a slight smirk on her face.

What is so funny? I thought. I was confused and scared. Several minutes later, my mother hung up the phone, expressed her sheer disappointment, and sharply told me to "get my behind upstairs" in that universal Black mother bravado that makes you quiver with fear.

Looking back, I now understand why my mother laughed. Despite the vulgar language, she realized my teacher was incredibly impressed with my artistic ability.

My talent was undeniable. Strangely, Mrs. V respected and praised my visual response to her persistent ridicule. Her description of the drawing had brought my mother to the point of uncontrollable laughter. She did not want to encourage my behavior, but as she held the drawing in her hands, she was also evidently blown away by the picture's detailed composition.

I was fortunate to have parents that advocated and fought for my well-being in every academic environment. They knew the challenges I would face as a young Black child, so they decided to do all they could to shepherd me through the system. I am grateful for their protection and their provision.

Unfortunately, for those who do not have advocates, their futures may be left in the hands of underpaid, culturally insensitive educators who look at disadvantaged children with low expectations and malicious intent.

This was and still is the norm in most inner-city public schools. They are a socioeconomic petri dish, full of lost hope and low expectations, a repository of dreams derailed by the rampant, unchecked false diagnoses that have stolen generations of melanated geniuses.

Without my parents vehemently advocating for me, I too may have fallen victim to a drug-induced suppression of my God-given ability.

They would have stopped my shine.

For the uninitiated, "shine" can be described as the radiance of God-given intelligence and purpose. For Black girls, we call this beautiful character trait "magic." This acknowledgment of our intrinsic value as Black people seeks to replenish what is stripped from us in the classroom, media, and workplace. It serves as a divine declaration of hope and self-acceptance.

This formative childhood experience taught me the importance of creating empathetic cultures in every academic and professional setting. I learned and understood we are not products of our environment. In actuality, we are products of the trauma and triumph we experience in our context. How you speak to someone can unlock potential or destroy their desire to commit fully.

Toxic leaders project their insecurities onto their direct reports or colleagues, much like toxic teachers who project biases onto unassuming students. I can only assume their authoritarian disposition masks a profound sense of hurt.

Ultimately, hurt leaders hurt organizations.

This is the primary reason talented people decide to exit roles and teams. The mission attracts them; poor leadership compels them to leave.

We are living through "The Great Resignation," a.k.a. "The Big Quit," a term coined by Anthony Klotz, a professor of management at Mays Business School of Texas A&M University. In 2021, amid a lagging economy, a global pandemic, and civic unrest, people were resigning at an alarming rate due to intolerable work environments, low wages, and profoundly inept leadership (Mann 2021).

Public declarations of inclusion have yet to reach the promise of a more equitable workplace. Now more than ever, people want to be accepted, heard, and treated with kindness. This should not be a controversial topic. It is all I wanted as a child in the classroom, and it is all anyone could want as a worker in their job.

To be a great creative leader, you must embrace a childlike, unfailing desire to see the world for what it could be. Kindness and empathy are the keys to unlocking trapped potential.

Ultimately, how we speak to one another in all settings truly matters.

Words bind to our being. So use them carefully and positively, and watch the world change around you.

Remember, the power of life and death resides in the words you speak about yourself and others.

CHAPTER 2

THE REAL-LIFE DR. LUCIUS FOX

People can only become what they see.

Representations of life in media, literature, history books, and art have been severely centered on a universal standard of elegance and eloquence that does not reflect the richness and cultural variety which make this world so beautiful. As a Black child, I struggled to find examples that celebrated the diversity of lived experiences in the community from which I came.

No multidimensional expression of Blackness was represented in the textbooks used to indoctrinate us into a culturally sanitized system of learning. Instead, we were left to find refuge and identity in pop culture icons that had seemingly transcended race and ethnicity to "arrive" at a place of prominence.

Their skill had provided them with an open invitation into predominately white spaces that saw them as singular beings who no longer belonged to the collective Black community.

They were “special Black,” meaning wealthy, famous, well-known, musical, or athletic.

In school, I was obviously not intellectually stimulated. I was bored, unchallenged, and an animated, hands-on learner. I needed to move and feel to understand. I learned by doing, not by listening, which brought more attention to my classroom behavior rather than my aptitude and ability. As a result, I was an easy target for discipline and chastising.

The solution was novel and compelling. My mother spoke with my second-grade teacher and convinced her to allow me to draw and/or color quietly when I finished my work before the rest of the class, which was often. This early diversion from a system that criminalized my natural behaviors sparked a desire to leverage drawing as a medium for self-expression and worth.

In my imagination, I was invincible. I was limitless. Drawing fueled my yearning for adventure and purpose.

I had found my thing.

It was not uncommon for me to rush home from school, eager to consume inspiring, imaginative content while exploring the boundaries of my creativity through various modalities of play. I loved it all. From playing Nintendo with my brother to chasing my sister around the house when we were supposed to be fast asleep, play invigorated me.

My vibrant personality was an extension of my play habits. Any changes in my mood, appetite, and energy were met with great concern. One evening, my mother noticed I was not engaged in my usual nightly antics. I commonly bounded across the hall to bother my little sister once my parents read her a book and gave her a kiss good night.

The typical sound of laughter and tiny feet lunging from our beds in defiance of our parents' rules had gone silent. In response to my lethargic state, my parents took me to the emergency room, but they sent us home with instructions to give me ibuprofen and monitor my temperature. That was not the outcome a concerned parent would settle for without hesitation.

We returned home, I was placed in bed, and the TV was turned to my favorite station. My parents comforted me with words of affirmation and care as they vigilantly watched me throughout the night.

"Everything will be okay. Just rest, Jason," my mother whispered as she ran her fingers through my curly dark brown hair.

Unfortunately, I struggled to rest.

All night I tossed and turned, sweated profusely, and groaned.

The next day, my parents decided to keep me home from school to monitor my progress closely. Unfortunately, as day turned to night, I still showed no improvement.

The nagging feeling of not knowing the cause of my ailment compelled my mother to place me beside her and my father so they could continue to watch over me lovingly. My parents were worried. I was barely moving, drained from a 104-degree fever, and utterly void of my typical youthful exuberance. I was worsening, and my mother felt a sense of urgency to act.

As I faded into unconsciousness, my father swept me up in his arms. He was a strong man of great character whose one purpose at that moment was to protect and care for his child. My mother and father gathered up their belongings and arranged for my grandmother to watch my siblings while they took me back to the emergency room of yet another hospital, hoping to find a cause for my illness.

It was a race against time, and they were determined to win.

We arrived at the hospital; my father opened the back passenger door of our dark obsidian-blue 1988 Toyota Camry, lifted me up with one arm, and closed the door with the other.

We hurried toward the entrance to the lobby of St. Francis Hospital, where we were directed to the elevators to proceed immediately up to the pediatric ward. My mother requested the aides call my pediatrician so he could help direct and engage the medical staff based on his knowledge of my health history.

He recommended a battery of tests intended to comprehensively scan for the source of my discomfort. He joined in the race against time and willingly became our anchor.

We waited patiently as the hospital staff reviewed and discussed the results. My parents prayed and remained poised despite intense despair. They were young, striving childhood sweethearts who had overcome tremendous adolescent adversity only to be again faced with a traumatic experience, this time with their own child.

The agony they felt was beyond words. Their faith would not stay idle in the face of tremendous emotional toil. But the circumstances did not cause dismay. They persevered, displaying the wisdom and conviction that come with love formed in the fire of tribulation.

Doubling down on their desire to see me well, they expected a clear answer and a set of recommended next steps. They demanded transparency. As the nurses approached us, my parents leaned forward, remaining calm and composed, eager to receive the results.

"Your son has septicemia. It's a blood infection," they shared, to my parents' surprise.

Septicemia, or sepsis, is the clinical name for bacterial blood poisoning. It is the body's most extreme response to an infection. Sepsis that progresses to septic shock has a death rate as high as 50 percent, depending on the type of organism involved (Johns Hopkins Medicine 2022).

Every second mattered.

Upon hearing the results, my pediatrician, Dr. Amin, asked that I be immediately transferred to South Suburban Hospital where he would oversee my treatment under his direct care.

We arrived and rushed through the lobby, onto the elevators, and up to the next pediatric ward. As the elevator doors opened, light rushed in and enveloped the silhouette of my arms draped over my father's broad shoulders. Our conjoined bodies cast a large shadow on the elevator's back wall. As we departed, I focused on the shadow, watching it fade as we walked away from the closing doors.

The floors were a sterile white laminate, softly glistening in the overhead fluorescent lights. The lobby was quiet and uneventful except for the late-night cleaning staff who were sanitizing the floors and common areas.

It was late, and we were tired, but my parents remained determined. I fiercely clung to life while trying to preserve my energy. But I faded in and out of awareness. I was scared and lethargic. I needed help immediately.

Dr. Amin sprinted toward my parents with the nursing staff in tow. They promptly placed me on a gurney, transported me to a room, and administered care while Dr. Amin explained to my parents the course of treatment I would undergo over the next several weeks.

He informed them I would need to receive a cocktail of antibiotics, steroids, and fluids intravenously while resting for ten to twelve hours daily. While he did not detect any damage to my vital organs, the infection had entered my bloodstream and would have killed me if my parents had not rushed me to the hospital. After the brief discussion, we settled into my room, and my parents took turns watching me rest throughout the night.

As the sun rose the following day, so did my father. He hesitantly departed for work after a long, sleepless night. He was forced to choose between standing by his wife and child and rushing off to work to protect our benefits and financial well-being. This choice is familiar to working-class families who experience medical emergencies. It's the unfortunate byproduct of a system that punishes poverty. My mother remained while my father went to work.

This routine would take place over the next few weeks with a series of rotating family members who all vowed to be by my side twenty-four hours daily until I could return home. My Uncle Fred, F.D., was especially committed. We shared a special bond in our comedic timing and sense of humor.

He was quick-witted, kindhearted, and spoke with extreme candor. He was the embodiment of being "unbothered." His presence provided comfort and entertainment. He would tease me to elicit a round of deep laughter followed by wheezing and coughing. He was determined to frame this memory as a positive one. He did not want me to be hurt and alone.

During the day, I was encouraged to move around to ensure my body got exercise. Often, my adventures would take me to the front desk, where I discovered I could have an unlimited supply of Pepsi Free if I consistently found ways to manipulate the nurse's affinity for children.

"*Que lindo*," she purred every time I approached the desk and lifted my head with a gaze like a puppy vying for attention.

"Can I please have another Pepsi Free?" I asked in a hushed tone.

She would immediately melt and send me back to my room. Later, she brought me a can of pop and a cup full of ice. These small moments of comfort went a long way toward healing my physical, psychological, and emotional trauma from what I was enduring.

In the early evening, I often walked down the hall, IV drip in tow, toward the playroom. Everything you could imagine was in that room, from Lincoln Logs to donated books. It was my break from the reality of the traumatic experience we were all facing.

This somber activity became the catalyst for who I am today. I was rummaging through an old pile of *Highlights* magazines when I came across this cover of *Batman* #307. I was excited to discover Batman was a comic book hero. Unfortunately, until then, my only exposure to the character was through the actor Adam West, who played Batman on TV.

Every Saturday, my father would take us to play basketball on the west side of Chicago, then we would stop to get some Chicago-style popcorn, a blend of cheddar- and caramel-coated kernels, and finally we would head home to watch *Batman*.

My curiosity compelled me to take the comic back to my room. To my surprise, the book introduced me to the true hero in the *Batman* story arc, Dr. Lucius Fox.

At the time, I didn't know that issue 307 marked his first appearance in the franchise.

As CEO and president of Wayne Enterprises and the Wayne Foundation, Lucius Fox is one of Bruce Wayne's closest allies. He is an experienced businessman, entrepreneur, and inventor who unknowingly runs the business interests that supply weapons, gadgets, vehicles, and armor for Bruce Wayne to use when he fights crime as the vigilante Batman.

He was an essential character who exuded power, intelligence, and ingenuity. He was also a Black man, just like my father.

This illustrated example of Black excellence convinced me I could be like Lucius, not Mike.

My hospital stay became much more bearable. I found a sense of wonder and joy in the pages of *Batman*. The art style, dialogue, and Dr. Fox's presence captivated my imagination.

I was healing and preparing for my inevitable discharge. When I was scheduled to depart, I packed up my belongings, hugged the nurse, and sprinted to the elevators.

I was going home.

Unfortunately, I do not remember what happened to the comic book. Did I leave it behind, bring it home, or simply forget it somewhere in the world? These questions I can never answer. Yet despite this unfortunate outcome, I am grateful for being exposed to the character of Dr. Lucius Fox during a critical time in my life.

His story has significantly influenced my career as a professional designer, educator, and entrepreneur. As a result, I have been able to inspire kids all over the world.

Dr. Lucius Fox expanded the possibility of what I could do with my curiosity and talent. Because of his example, I aspire to impact the lives of creative youth through care, creativity, and wise counsel, much like Dr. Fox's work with a young Bruce Wayne.

Even superheroes need a mentor.

CHAPTER 3

WALKING BAREFOOT THROUGH THE GRASS

The preciousness of now is fleeting.

As life slips through our hands like grains of sand, we desperately try to hold on to our most vivid experiences while letting go of the moments we fall short. We strive to define our lives by beautiful memories and meaningful connections.

During crucial moments of adolescent growth, the negative impact of wasted time becomes an ever-present reality. For me, transitioning from elementary school to middle school and middle school to high school only heightened the awareness of my youth fading away. I wanted to grow up but did not want to grow older.

From my sixth grade start in 1991 to middle school graduation in 1994, my classmates and I changed from children to prepubescent teenagers. The world saw us as future victims; we saw ourselves as future success stories.

I would often hang around friends who shared my desire to discuss Batman while reveling in the imaginative innocence of our youth. But as we grew, our interests shifted toward debates about our favorite athletes or most creative hip-hop groups, not long-winded descriptions of fictitious characters.

Going into middle school, our appetite for adventure grew in proportion to the feeling of our perceived newfound freedom. We would traverse our neighborhood on bikes as if we were auditioning to become the Black Goonies. Our world was rapidly expanding beyond the watchful eye of our parents and families.

Unlike most of my friends at the time, I was fortunate to have a stable home life and a deep, loving relationship with my parents and grandparents. They accepted me with my unique interests and different learning style. As a result, I did not have to pretend to be someone I was not to find love at home.

During middle school, I spent significant amounts of time with my mother's side of the family. Her siblings and mother all moved closer together as they grew older.

They strived to create a strong family bond through proximity, and we, the children and grandchildren, benefitted greatly from their presence. At the head of the family was my grandmother, who we affectionately called "Bootsie."

She was a phenomenal woman. Her essence was divinity in human form.

She exuded a strength in her being that allowed her to leverage humor to disarm anyone who dared bring negativity into her presence. She commanded respect and adoration as the matriarch of our family and, in most cases, in any room in which she stood. Her laugh was sweet and deep. She loved us thoroughly. Her love was evident in how her beautiful honey-toned skin radiated joy as she smiled. She genuinely acknowledged the value of those around her. To know Grandma Bootsie was to understand pure love.

Before my eighth grade year ended, my grandmother was diagnosed with brain cancer. The news of her condition profoundly impacted the lives of her children. Our world was shifting tremendously fast.

The head of our family was potentially facing the end of her life, and she was at peace. Her faith in God had provided comfort during a time of fear and uncertainty. Despite the news, she remained committed to spending all her time with us. In her last months of life, she consistently searched for clever ways to be closer to her grandchildren.

Her commitment to living every remaining moment with joy was no surprise to my parents, aunts, and uncles. Her love for her family, especially her grandchildren, kept her alive. As a young woman, she had dreamed of being an educator. She wanted to empower children through knowledge and compassion. Strangely, her battle with cancer had provided her with a chance to live out a portion of her dream.

During chemotherapy, she began volunteering in my middle school cafeteria to protect me from the unkempt kitchen staff, who she often called "nasty a——s heifers."

Every afternoon, she would arrive early, walk confidently to the cafeteria, and prepare for my arrival.

"Here you go, baby," she would say with a smile as she placed a healthier portion of food onto my tray.

"Thank you so much, Grandma. I love you," I said, then returned to my table to break bread with my friends.

After school, she would return to her apartment to sit for hours, browsing the pages of *Reader's Digest* and laughing at reruns of her favorite shows. For a short period, this became her new routine.

Despite her fighting spirit and frequent chemotherapy, her health gradually faded. Her skin lost its glow. Her hair withered away, and the hope of her survival dwindled.

My mother and her siblings prepared themselves for the worst. They catered to her every need immediately. During the outpatient care process, my grandmother shared with her children that she wanted to recreate a precious memory from her childhood. Her wish was simple and sweet. She dreamed of walking barefoot through the grass one last time.

My aunts, uncles, and parents obliged and met to decide on a location and time. While they sat and organized her outing, my young mind remained fixated on reconnecting with my friends for a casual bike ride to the local baseball card shop. We were searching for a Jason Kidd rookie card, and nothing, not even going to the park with my grandma, would stop us.

Despite my brush with death years earlier, my adolescent consciousness could not comprehend the moment's importance. Although surprisingly she did not force me to go, she understood and appreciated the desire of a child's heart. Her innocent request was equal to my own.

"It's okay, baby. Have fun with your friends," she said as I hugged her and sprinted toward the door.

No one could predict her visit to the park would be one of her last moments in the sun.

Unfortunately, my desire to be with friends caused me to miss my last chance to form a core memory with Grandma Bootsie. The thought of seeing my grandma alive and joyful for the last time had not crossed my mind.

A few days later, she returned to the hospital due to cancer complications. Her health speedily decreased, and she slipped into a coma, causing her to pass away quietly and peacefully in her sleep.

I immediately and deeply regretted my selfish act. How could I be so stupid? Why didn't I go to the park with her? These questions plagued my mind for the entire summer before I entered high school.

She lived long enough to see me graduate from eighth grade, and I was confident she would also live to see my brother graduate. I was, regrettably, wrong in my assumption.

The inner hurt and anguish from missing her last moment in the sun led me to act out in anger and sadness. Over time, I engaged in activities that could have cost me my freedom and, ultimately, my life.

My circle of friends changed, and I slipped into a cycle of mischievousness in pursuit of "feeling" again. Her passing broke my heart and my spirit. My imagination had led me to believe she was too strong to die and I was too young to sit still at the moment. Both mindsets were grossly inaccurate.

Looking back now, I realize I was emotionally fragile—vibrating with an energy that attracted spirits intent on feeding on my despair. Blinded by my sadness, I could not discern who was praying for me and who was preying on me in my time of need.

While grieving the loss of my grandmother, I befriended two boys, Nate and Jamarcus. They were charismatic, well-dressed, and seemingly popular cousins that had just moved into our neighborhood. We grew closer in a matter of weeks and formed a bond. We were inseparable, and their lifestyle fascinated me.

The way they dressed, spoke, and carried themselves was awe-inspiring. Despite their limited financial resources, they always found a way to have the latest shoes, clothes, and video game consoles. These symbolic examples of cultural relevance afforded them a position of influence in our neighborhood in a relatively short time.

It would not be long before a simple conversation revealed the source of their abundance.

"Hey, tell the truth, how do you always have new stuff?" I asked innocently.

"My mom steals all of this stuff, man. She hit a lick and came up at Kmart. She flipped the rest," Jamarcus replied. He was proud of his mother's hustle.

"Word? For real? How did she steal Jordans? They don't sell those at Kmart!" I asked in sheer disbelief.

They burst into uncontrollable laughter and dismissed my comment as too intrusive.

"G, we're not telling you that, man," Nate responded. "Do you want something? Just ask. We got you." He turned his back and walked toward the side entrance to his home.

Despite the apparent warning signs, I declined politely and continued to spend time with them frequently. We would walk to school together during the week and play basketball around the city on the weekends.

During one weekend adventure, an impromptu pickup basketball game at a friend's house transformed into a home invasion. They overheard our friend mention he and his family were driving to Wisconsin Dells, a popular Midwest water park destination, for the weekend. So, naturally, this was their opportunity to rummage through his collection of video games, shoes, and other precious keepsakes that adorned the shelves and walls of the home.

After playing a quick game of twenty-one, they suggested we enter the home through a basement window to retrieve a video game they claimed they had accidentally left behind the previous day.

"You coming? The window may be unlocked. Let's check it." Nate pointed toward the small rectangular window adjacent to the back patio.

"Uh, okay." I had accepted their invitation to enter the home, and I knew it was a mistake. My desire to be their friend blinded my judgment. A false sense of belonging was filling the void in my heart from the loss of my grandmother. They didn't care about me. They only wanted to see how far they could push me beyond my comfort zone. Their plan was premeditated. It was a setup, and I did not even know it.

I felt overwhelming apprehension as we descended into the basement through the window. I was not where I was supposed to be at that moment, and I knew it.

How did I slip so far into the pit of self-pity as to be persuaded to transgress against a neighbor?

Yet, despite my feelings, my body continued to move forward. Before my feet could touch the ground, they had entered the room, sprinted up the stairs, and begun to scavenge with the intensity of a military raid.

Nothing was left unturned.

I was scared to see what they had done. At that moment, I decided this was not what I wanted to do. I knew I had to leave.

With sweat dripping from my forehead, I clung to the window's ledge, lifted myself off the ground, and slid back through the open window. Then, in a panic, I jumped on my bike and rushed to where I thought I would be safe, my uncle Tony's house, about a mile from the crime scene.

I was overcome with fear for hours whenever my uncle's phone rang.

Was anyone looking for me?

Did someone see me?

Was I in trouble?

Day turned to early evening, and the phone rang once more. The fate I had been hoping to avoid was upon me.

"Where the hell is Jason?" I could hear the anger in my mother's voice.

"Right here. Let me put him on the phone," my uncle Tony replied.

"Hello?" I said with a tremble in my voice.

"Get your a--s home *right now*. The police are here. *Get home now.*"

She informed my uncle that Nate and Jamarcus were spotted leaving the home and apprehended shortly afterward. Coincidentally, the arresting officer was my cousin. According to their statements, I was the mastermind who had physically intimidated them into committing an unlawful act against their will. Upon hearing my name, he immediately called my mother to inform her I was potentially a suspect in a nearby home invasion case.

My uncle hung up the phone, gathered my belongings, and drove me back home, where I was cuffed and placed in the back of a waiting squad car.

Witnessing the tears streaming down my mother's face as another family member hauled me off for interrogation was the lowest moment of my life. My entire future was in jeopardy, and I had no one to blame but myself.

The three of us were separated and placed in different rooms upon arrival. While interrogated, Nate and Jamarcus had disguised their criminal intent with performative tears and pleas for forgiveness. They both took turns blaming me for the incident. They believed my life was disposable—a means to an end.

Their stories placed the blame squarely on my shoulders. For over an hour, I sat in silence, alone, cuffed to a cold, stainless steel table in an all-white room while they individually provided contradictory accounts of my involvement.

I felt like cattle awaiting slaughter, cuffed to the table in a space designed to make you feel caught by the devil's lasso. Then, finally, the door burst open and my cousin entered the room, uncuffed my hand from the table, and brought me into a larger space where my two former friends sat together with their hands cuffed while his partner stood in silence nearby.

"So tell us what happened again," his partner asked them rhetorically. He flexed his hand, wearing a black leather glove.

Before they could answer, he slapped them across the face with the force of a man who intended to inflict fear.

I stared, frozen, as I witnessed two young Black boys unjustly treated like savages.

We were all just trying to survive. Our actions were misguided and dangerous, but the punishment felt brutal.

They begged him to stop as he repeatedly struck them.

"Tell us. Tell us what really happened!" he shouted.

Each blow broke their spirit and, ultimately, mine. Then, pleading for mercy, they confessed.

"Please, please, please. Jason didn't do anything, man, d——n. *Please.* He left, man. He left!"

Their confession momentarily absolved me of my involvement in the crime they had committed. But nevertheless, I had entered the home, and I was still considered an accomplice in the eyes of the law.

Hours after their confession, I was processed, released into the care of my father, and given a court date. We immediately drove to the home where the incident had occurred, and my father firmly walked me to the door to speak with our neighbors.

I was ashamed and humiliated.

My actions had caused harm beyond comprehension. I apologized profusely and vowed to repay them for any damage I may have caused.

The same people I had transgressed against recognized me. I did not have the emotional capacity to advocate for myself, yet they showed me great mercy and understanding. They knew me from my entrepreneurial endeavors. They saw me as the "kid in the neighborhood who would cut your grass and shovel your snow."

They understood I was struggling with grief from my grandmother's passing and I had made a severe mistake choosing to associate with people with a history of criminal behavior. They did not press charges, and more importantly, they forgave me.

I exhaled a sigh of relief as we walked back down their stairs, across the street, and into our car. I felt redeemed but unsure if the judge would feel the same.

Weeks later, on the day of my hearing, I felt the overwhelming presence of my grandmother Bootsie all around me. But the biggest blessing was when I noticed the bailiff on duty was the grandmother of my younger cousin, Jeremy.

Officer Roby had been close to my Grandma Bootsie—her son my aunt Michelle's husband, my grandma's second daughter. She had known me since I was a baby and understood Grandma Bootsie's death profoundly impacted me.

Her presence comforted me in a difficult moment. Officer Roby stood side by side with the judge as he scolded me for my behavior and expressed how disappointed so many people would be if I ended up in jail for a senseless, avoidable circumstance.

I stood emotionally broken, and my father nudged me to look the judge in the eyes and receive my punishment like a man.

"I am not going to ruin your life today, young man. Too many people believe in your dream. Too many people have advocated on your behalf. They tell me you want to design shoes for Michael Jordan. Is this true?

"Yes, sir. Yes. I want to work at Nike one day."

"Do you think this is the way to get there?"

"No, sir."

My desire to be the real-life Lucius Fox led me to believe Michael Jordan was Chicago's own Bruce Wayne. I would tell anyone who would listen that one day, I would "grow up to design shoes for Michael Jordan." As a superhero, those were his weapons of choice, and in my mind, I would one day be the person responsible for creating them.

"You're lucky. I'm tired, and I'm not going to do this today. I'm keeping your name in my ledger, and if I ever see you in here again, I will charge you, no questions asked. The next time I see you, I better get a pair of the shoes you designed. Understand?"

"Yes, sir," I replied before collapsing into my father's arms, overcome by relief.

He had given me a second chance. The dream that started during my battle with septicemia had given me my freedom. As an adult, I now believe my grandmother's spirit was present with me that day.

Her profound example of strength in her final days taught me to remain grounded despite my circumstances and to cling to the unbeatable feeling of childlike joy in moments of worry and despair.

Grandma Bootsie taught me to be present and to feel the world around me at all times.

In our moments of honest vulnerability, yearning to belong, we can truly experience freedom.

Looking back, I learned a precious lesson from my brush with the law.

The pain of socioeconomic strife made destructive behaviors attractive to my friends. The rebellious acts of their youth were expressions of frustration and unaddressed trauma. They had come from abusive homes where deceit was normalized and theft was a way of life.

They were not acting up; they were crying out for help. Unfortunately, people judge others' behaviors before attempting to understand their pain. As I've grown, I've developed a profound empathy for others.

Studies have shown that child maltreatment roughly doubles the probability that an individual engages in various criminal activities (Picker 2007).

Nate and Jamarcus were victims, and no one ever attempted to understand what caused them to engage in dangerous behaviors at such a young age. No one ever gave them the benefit of the doubt.

I would never see my friends again after our final day together in court. I was not allowed to socialize with anyone outside my home for the remainder of the school year. My parents feared I was heading in the wrong direction and, if left alone, I would end up dead or in jail.

They were unsuccessful despite their attempts to shield me from the world's ways.

Months later, I was witness to a more severe crime.

A simple argument between two of my closest friends from middle school carried into high school and resulted in a tragic incident that lasted one hundred and eighty seconds.

My life would soon change forever.

CHAPTER 4

ONE HUNDRED AND EIGHTY SECONDS

Trauma creates angst in the heart and mind of a developing child.

In the fall of 1994, an event that lasted one hundred and eighty seconds became the catalyst for my evolution into the person I am today.

After experiencing a brush with the law months earlier, I was not allowed to spend meaningful time with friends outside of our typical school day activities. However, this absence from my usual social circles only partially removed me from our flow of daily communication.

During gym, lunch, and in between classes, I would learn of the latest conflicts, relationships, and upcoming social events. So I was not surprised when I heard two of my closest friends, Keith and Donte, were at odds. A simple misunderstanding between them rapidly escalated into a highly anticipated confrontation.

Tension mounted for days as rumors of their brewing conflict spread like wildfire among our peer groups.

One morning as we waited to enter the gym to train before classes started, Donte burst into the locker room, enraged.

"Ooh, I'm gonna beat his a——s when I see him!" he exclaimed as he turned the corner.

His booming voice traveled throughout the locker room and spilled into the hallway where Veronica, Keith's cousin, stood waiting to enter the gym.

Keith and Donte shared a similar physical stature and disposition. They were equally athletic and brave; however, Keith had a "wolf" mentality. He believed violence was law, and he would tolerate no act of disrespect.

Donte continued to speak, each word getting more pronounced and fueled with rage as he exited the locker room onto the basketball court.

He felt violated by a hard foul he received from Keith during a pickup basketball game earlier in the week. In his mind, Keith's actions were intentional. By speaking loudly, Donte guaranteed that Veronica would hear his threat and respond with force in Keith's absence.

She rushed toward him. "Whose a——s you gonna beat? Not my cousin; he'll kill yo a——s. I put that on everything."

The crowd of students drew closer to Donte and Veronica and responded in unison, "Ooh."

Immediately, I intervened, trying my best to extinguish the tension between my peers.

"Chill, fam, chill. It's not that deep. It happened, it was an accident, and it's already been a week, man. Let it go," I said, hoping to de-escalate the situation.

"Naw, G. That man threw the ball at my face *after* he fouled me. That ain't on accident. He been a hater since he thought I tried to holla at his girl," Donte responded dismissively.

At that moment, Veronica darted across the court toward the exit doors. "Just wait. He coming to get yo a——s after school. Watch." Her words silenced the entire gym for a brief moment. We understood she was on her way to inform Keith of Donte's grievance, and things would undoubtedly turn violent.

Despite numerous attempts to resolve conflict peacefully throughout the week, my beloved brothers raged against the idea that they could have solved their disagreement through discourse rather than a physical altercation.

When all you have is your name, you protect it fiercely. The Chicago we lived in and its divisive media, failed school systems, and hidden caste system stripped us of our worth. Students at Chicago's lowest-performing high schools drop out at nearly twelve times the rate of average Illinois students—36 percent compared to 3 percent. Lack of resources and opportunity placed a significant premium on respect as a form of social currency (Illinois Policy 2013).

We lived by a code of honor.

An honor-based culture, or "a culture in which a person (usually a man) feels obliged to protect his or her reputation by answering insults, affronts, and threats, often through the use of violence," is typical in most socioeconomically challenging environments (Psychology 2016).

Their mutual veiled threats, disrespectful remarks, and dehumanizing tones caused Keith and Donte to choose confrontation over reconciliation. The code of the streets dictated that if neither decided to respond with force, the entire school would view them as weak and unworthy of respect.

As the day progressed, a series of probing questions awaited me in every class.

"What happened, G? I heard it's about to pop off after school?"

"I hope not, man. We can't be on that. We're fam. I hope they figure it out." Everyone present knew the tone of my response was uncertain.

They urged me to intercede quickly. They knew Keith and Donte were under the influence of the honor code we had all been born into without our consent.

Through their provocation, I feverishly searched for my friends that day to no avail. Unfortunately, Keith was serving a two-week suspension for a previous fight, and it would be virtually impossible for me to reach Donte in time due to conflicting schedules.

The day came to a close, and I rushed from my final class to where the fight would take place, behind a Rent-A-Center in an empty parking lot directly across from our school's front entrance. I had convinced myself that if I could reach one of them in time, my love and respect for them would neutralize the disagreement.

Nervously, I approached the parking lot and spotted Keith standing next to a black 1985 Buick Regal with twenty-inch rims and tinted windows, accompanied by two older gangsters from the neighborhood. Moving slowly, with hesitation and concern, I approached Keith and pled my case to resolve their disagreement amicably.

"Please, man. Just go home, G. Please."

Nothing I said seemed to chip away at the cold, eerie sense of calm Keith expressed on his face. It was as if he knew this moment would end our friendship.

He grabbed me by my shoulder, smiled, and said, "Jay, calm down; I want to talk to him, man. It's all good." I knew what he was inferring at that moment. Violence was the only way forward.

As a small crowd gathered behind us, there was a noticeable increase in chatter.

Something was happening.

Before I could spring into action, Donte rushed to the front of the crowd, ready to defend his honor. His facial expression showed me he had prepared for a fight.

"What's up now, man? You said you was gonna see me; here I am, bruh? *What's good, man?*" Donte shouted as he broke through the crowd, instantly placing me in the center of their conflict.

I was alone, trapped in the middle, left to physically separate them as the crowd urged them toward a violent outcome.

Keith placed his hand on my shoulder again; his eerie sense of calm had now transformed into a menacing smile. In an instant, he forcefully moved me to the side. From my peripheral view, I saw a gun.

Bang!

He fired one shot into Donte's cheek, a young Black man that was ill-prepared for what he was to encounter that day. The bullet ripped the flesh from the right side of Donte's face, leaving a gaping wound the size of a golf ball.

In an instant, I went into shock.

The crowd dispersed as the gun pointed toward them with one firm declaration. "Jason was not here, right? Jason was never here." His words were Keith's attempt to protect me from his wrongdoing.

It was his way of showing me love. He decided my future was more valuable than his own. He appreciated my passion for art and often encouraged me to share my shoe drawings with the world. He believed in me, even when I did not believe in myself.

I vaguely remember clutching my left breast jacket pocket amid the chaos of screams and students running for safety.

In that left jacket pocket, I typically carried a sketch of a shoe on a torn piece of lined paper. The subject of the sketch was always my interpretation of the latest Air Jordan. Over the years, I fell in love with the idea that drawing shoes was my identity, my way of being seen.

Keith grabbed my shoulder again, shaking me violently to wake me from my shock-induced paralysis. His action instantly brought me back to consciousness.

"Run, G. Run!"

Keith had accepted his fate would be like many of our fallen kings and queens. So he had chosen the way of the streets.

Overcome with fear, I ran as fast as possible toward the only place I felt safe, the local Foot Locker, about a block from where the shooting occurred.

It was my place of refuge. It was my place of peace. It was where I would sit and sketch shoes I admired but could never afford. Conveniently located at the far end of the school's parking lot, it had become a familiar neutral territory.

As I fled through the parking lot, my brow was drenched in sweat, masking the tears streaming down my face. I decided to stop ten yards from the entrance to wipe my face with a balled-up gym shirt buried underneath hastily gathered class materials at the bottom of my backpack.

I fought to control my breath as I placed my hand on the cold, weathered door handle. Entering the store provided an overwhelming sense of relief. I darted toward the wall of shoes and avoided all eye contact with other patrons.

The sales associate approached me, flashing a curious smile. "You were here the other day drawing Mikes, right?"

I stood frozen, assuming he would ask me to leave. "Uh, yeah. I was. Is it cool if I finish?" I said with a tone of bewilderment. I was shocked anyone had noticed me sketching Jordans. In my mind, I was covertly capturing the details of each artifact displayed prominently on the wall of innovation I had come to love.

"All love, G. I think it's dope! Just sit over there and stay out of the way. You need to get up if someone needs to try on a shoe. We good?"

"We good," I replied as I walked calmly to the bench, sat down, retrieved my notebook from my backpack, and sketched shoes for the next few hours.

I lost myself in the paper's grain as my pencil spilled elements of my imagination onto the page. Every line had given me life. My frantic desire to sketch provided a feeling of peace in my unsettled spirit.

The only thing that calmed me down at that moment was sitting and drawing Jordans, or Mikes, as we like to call them in Chicago.

I sketched with the desire to find a way out of my circumstances. I had barely escaped incarceration the previous summer, and now this. I needed a way out.

Creativity would become my jump shot.

The sun had begun to set over the city, and a calm tone had overtaken the world beyond the walls of Foot Locker. Long after the crowds dispersed, the cries of the sirens rushing to my friend's aid echoed in my mind.

Prepared to depart, I was determined to get home safely. Three hours had passed, my older brother had already left school before the fight, and my parents were on their way home from work. I could not delay my journey home. It was time.

I rose, wiping the eraser shavings from my clothes, gathered my belongings, dapped up the manager, and threw on my jacket and backpack. I felt like a soldier deployed into combat.

The walk home gave me time to gather my composure. I was determined never to let my parents know what I had witnessed. I wanted it to all go away.

The next day in school, rumors swirled. "I heard he got hit like five times!" someone whispered as I walked through the hallway toward my locker.

Like most socioeconomically disadvantaged schools, we did not have adequate support for students who experienced trauma.

Each malignant experience forced us to self-medicate. Some of us turned to hyper-promiscuity, others turned to drugs, and a few leaned further into our academic, artistic, or athletic interests.

The rest accepted our reality would be one of conflict and pain with the occasional fleeting moment of joy.

Each child had their own experience with this abnormal fact of our lives.

Where the district fell short, the teachers stood in the gap. Mr. Summers was one of those teachers who cared deeply. He was aware of what we had witnessed and decided to create an intentional place of peace for us all.

A dedicated art teacher, husband, and father, he consistently encouraged us to pour our pain into our craft. He exposed us to pottery, fine art, sculpture, and illustration. However, airbrushing became our hustle of choice. Paasche Gravity Feed Airbrushes replaced spray cans, and sketchbooks served as look-books for our clients. He provided the space and resources, allowing us to monetize our talent. He offered an alternative to our reality without expecting reciprocity.

The day came to a close, and Mr. Summers found me in the hallway and reminded me we had an art club meeting after school. He wanted me there early to help organize the new paint that had just arrived. Each art student customarily earned access to supplies by volunteering to clean and organize the supply room. So after a few weeks of shadowing a classmate, my turn finally came to work in his office and learn the names, prices, and utility of each piece of art equipment he had acquired from years of teaching.

"No doubt, Mr. Summers. I'll be there fo sho," I exclaimed without breaking stride on my way to my final class of the day.

When I arrived at his classroom, Mr. Summers was on the phone; we made eye contact, and he waved me toward the back. However, he was visibly agitated, so I responded with a nod and walked promptly to the back office to begin work.

When I entered the office, I noticed Mr. Summers had left his personal belongings on the desk for all to see.

What in the hell is he thinking? I thought.

His wallet, a worn brown leather billfold, lay exposed on the desk. The bulging pile of receipts, twenty-dollar bills, and credit cards gave me pause. Then, fearing someone might accuse me of stealing his wallet, I left the room to alert him of his unassuming blunder.

"What are you doing?" he said in a deep, authoritative tone, appearing out of nowhere.

"Mr. Summers, what are *you* doing? Do you know who we are? Why did you leave your wallet out, man? You buggin'!" I replied, disgusted by his lack of regard for our freedom.

Without hesitation and with great confusion, Mr. Summers responded, "What? Are you crazy? You're not a criminal; you're a *kid*. Now get back to work. I trust you. Get back to work."

His nonchalant attitude toward the matter revealed society had tricked me into only seeing myself as a potential threat. My mere existence served as an analogy for criminality.

He was the embodiment of empathy. As a middle-aged white man from Chicago, stout with a thick auburn mustache and a spirited Midwestern accent, he saw me as a child, full of potential and talent, just like his own. So he gave me the benefit of the doubt.

His gracious act gave me my first taste of self-governance and responsibility. Finally, someone trusted me and saw the potential and power beneath my fragile exterior. He saw I was simply a kid who loved to draw sneakers. He believed in my dream. He believed in me.

I visited Mr. Summers's classroom every day for the rest of the year. On the days I could not catch a ride home with my brother, he would allow me to airbrush the sketches I created during my daily visits to Foot Locker. I explored different mediums, techniques, and styles with his guidance.

Art saved me. Art gave me a voice.

Traumatic experiences form the foundation of our boundaries and our fears. They can be our teachers or our captors.

When interacting with people from all walks of life, I remind myself of Mr. Summers's kind act. I assume that, much like me, they are operating from a place of pain, masking their wounds under the guise of professionalism.

The tragedy and triumph of that day never left me. The pain of that experience gave me PTSD and anxiety that lasted well into my adult life. I have overcome the pain embedded within my subconscious mind through introspection, prayer, therapy, fitness, and meditation. Because of this shadow memory, I strive to be a man of compassion and empathy rather than anger and double-mindedness. I hold on to the preciousness of each moment, seizing any opportunity to encourage and inspire.

Donte survived the attack with a small scar where the bullet exited his cheek. He would eventually give his life to God, who directed his path forward with more care and discernment for when his ego would compel him to fight. The scar on his cheek forever reminds him of his awakening and the resurrection of his identity and self-worth. Violence strangely gave him life.

Unfortunately, Keith's life continued to spiral into crime, violence, and incarceration.

Keith's conscious decision to protect me from his violent act ended my desire to rebel against the world after years of feeling the sting of peer rejection. In turn, I shifted my focus from belonging to pursuing my dream of designing shoes for Michael Jordan.

As time went on, we continued to grow further apart. Eventually, we lost touch with one another and never looked back.

Those hundred and eighty seconds were the last time we would all be together.

CHAPTER 5

PEOPLE CAN ONLY BECOME WHAT THEY SEE

Dreams become goals when you give them a deadline.

My most excellent teachers are the ambiguity, uncertainty, and faith required to endure change. Faith enables you to run toward fate confidently, knowing all things are in harmony with your purpose when you move at the speed of grace. Change is an inevitable experience in life.

However, growth as a result of the change is optional.

Those who embrace the discomfort of ambiguity enjoy outcomes beyond their imagination. Life's arduous tests form the foundation of our testimonies.

My test came in the summer of 1997 during my senior year of high school. My parents decided to relocate as a preventive measure to protect my younger sister from the failing school system my brother and I attended.

Our neighborhood had worsened, gun violence increased, and access to academic resources declined. As a result, the community was no longer a place of belonging and culture. Instead, it devolved into a disparate network of dilapidated homes, gang affiliations, and limited opportunities for advancement.

We toed the line between poverty and providence like many Black families growing up in Chicago. We did not have a lot, but we had what we needed.

We needed sanctuary and safe passage to our institutions of learning. So my parents chose to move our family to a small, diverse middle-class south suburb of Chicago. There, I would reconnect with Lasar, a dear friend from middle school who had returned from Louisiana to finish his final high school years up north.

Our reconnection was no coincidence. We shared a passion for art and sports and were both highly competitive and comedic. We spent our days discussing plans for our futures and finding ways to integrate ourselves into the school's established culture.

Being the new kid is never a pleasant experience. Being the new kid in your senior year is exponentially worse. Teachers have no interest in mentoring you because they have no established relationship, nor do they have a historical understanding of your learning and behavior patterns beyond transcripts.

Each day, your classmates screen you for undesirable traits to assign you to either the cool kids' table or to eat alone with the "othered" students.

Thankfully, because of my exceptional academic standing and work ethic, I spent most of my day in the athletic director's office alongside my track-and-field coach and other college-bound student athletes.

During the second part of my day, I worked in the art studio, practicing and refining my craft in hopes of finding an academic environment that encouraged creativity and self-expression.

I longed to surround myself with curious students who wanted to serve humanity's greatest needs with their designed products. I knew this environment would be perfect for a kid who wanted to become the real-life Dr. Lucius Fox.

Until then, I had assumed I needed to be an engineer to design products. But I had not yet become aware of the various disciplines beyond engineering that contributed heavily to the product-creation process. As a result, I had a limited view of how I would achieve my goal.

"I'm going to design footwear for Michael Jordan one day," I frequently proclaimed to my peers, coaches, and academic advisor.

Creativity had become my jump shot, my way out of my circumstances, and they were there to ensure I played at the highest level. My coach and principal were impressed with the clarity and passion of my personal goal.

They encouraged me with information and space to create. They pushed me toward my dreams by engaging in affirming and supportive discourse. They wanted to see me win.

Similarly, my mother was also aware of my desire to design products for Jordan. She fed me with articles, store visitations, and an unfailing willingness to listen to my wild visions for my future. Through my sharing, she grew a heightened sense of awareness for the industry I loved and would routinely find unique, inspirational stories to help me see my dream was valid.

During a routine trip to the grocery store, she noticed a *Chicago Sun-Times* auto show edition. The front page displayed a beautiful image of a Toyota concept vehicle and an accompanying story about the young designer who had, as the article mentioned, also interned at Nike. She immediately grabbed the newspaper and brought it home to share with me as soon as I arrived from school.

Simultaneously, my coach had also seen the article and remembered our long talks about my desire to design for Nike, and he also bought a copy to hand me at school the next day.

The universe had conspired to provide me the next step in my journey.

This move to a new community brought my sister and me more than a safe environment. My mother and coach's divine inclination provided me with fertile ground—a place where my dreams would flourish rather than suffocate.

God had given me the next clue in the mystery of my purpose.

I devoured the article, scanning for terminology, names, contact information, and anything that could give me more insight into how this student obtained that opportunity.

Where did he attend college?

What was his major?

What do you need to get an internship?

These questions infiltrated my thoughts and invigorated my spirit.

They gave shape to my identity. Then, finally, after years of writing letters to Nike and piecing together information from Foot Locker, I found a way. I finally knew how to become the person I dreamed I could become.

I needed to become an intern.

When I arrived at school the next day, Coach Daniels asked me to meet him in his office, and he handed me a copy of the article.

"Thank you! My mom saw this as well," I replied. With a tone of cautious optimism, I asked, "Coach Daniels, what should I do? This is so dope, but I need to figure out where to start."

"Call Toyota. Ask them to tell you where that kid went to school. That's what you should do. Keep calling until you get the answer you need to move forward. You got this, son. Keep seeking," he responded with certainty and care.

The prophetic words of a compassionate Black man gave me everything I needed at that moment to overcome my fear. Next, I needed to learn to advocate for myself to advance academically and professionally.

I gathered my thoughts, turned on the office computer, and searched for information that would put me in touch with Toyota.

Much to my surprise, the corporate headquarters in Japan listed their general number on their website. Unfortunately, I was unaware of international time zones, and I picked up the phone and called on a Friday afternoon in the US, which was early Saturday morning in Japan.

I left a message explaining I wanted to get in touch with someone who could provide insight about their design internships. I did not expect a call or a message in return but hoped to get one step closer to achieving my dreams.

When I returned to school on Monday, Coach Daniels called me into the athletic director's office.

"Hey, champ. Do you know you called Japan on Friday?" Coach Daniels asked with a smirk on his face.

"Yeah, you told me to reach out for more info. So I did. Did I do something wrong?" I responded.

"Well, I am taking some heat for the charges. But it don't matter. You got a call back, and they left you a message. So it is what it is. Proud of you, boy!"

To my surprise, an executive from Toyota's design team offered to speak with me when he visited the United States the following week. I stood in silence, shocked. I had taken the first step in using my voice. I had manifested a way forward, and I could either lean into my dreams and return the call or become the weapon formed against me and cower in fear.

I wrote down the email shared in his voice mail, gathered my thoughts, and replied in writing with my sincerest gratitude for what the executive had offered to do.

When the day came for us to speak, I was nervous but determined. He was visiting their design studio in Southern California and informed me he only had a limited amount of time for me.

As we spoke, I bombarded him with questions.

"Where did the intern in the article go to school?"

"What was his major?"

"What is it like being a designer?"

His responses were sharp and insightful.

"Well, there is ArtCenter in Pasadena and College for Creative Studies in Detroit. To design shoes, I would suspect you may want to look into industrial design. Where do you live, by the way? How old are you?" he asked.

"I'm seventeen, and I live in Chicago. South side. Well, now the south suburbs. So basically Chicago."

"Wow!" he said.

He was shocked to find out I was a seventeen-year-old kid from the south side of Chicago who had tracked him down via the early internet.

"To tell you the truth, ArtCenter is expensive, the average student age is twenty-five, and it is competitive. Also, they don't have dorms, so it's quite hard for someone so young with no family in California. So here is what I would do if I were you . . ."

I held my breath in anticipation of his wisdom.

"If I were you, I would go to CCS."

He continued, "It's a phenomenal school in Detroit, only a few hours from Chicago, and if you fail out of industrial design, it would be easier to drive home than to fly back from LA."

I was not afraid of failure; I was scared to remain in Chicago and fall victim to the circumstances of my environment. However, due to our call, the phrase industrial design piqued my interest, and I was more determined than ever to become an ID student.

We hung up the phone, and I searched for more information about CCS.

Eventually, I stumbled upon CCS's website, admissions email address, and a form to request a tangible book highlighting the various majors, disciplines, and educational experiences afforded to students who survived the rigorous portfolio submission process.

After ordering the book, I checked our mailbox daily. I was as eager to receive the prospective student handbook as I was for my *Eastbay* catalog. Both items fed my curiosity and understanding of the footwear industry.

The day had finally come, and my mom lovingly placed the booklet on our kitchen table for me to discover when I returned home from school.

“You got some mail today, Jason. It’s on the table,” she announced as I walked through the door.

“From who? CCS?” I asked, dropping my backpack on the floor and then hustling toward the kitchen table.

It had finally arrived. I tore open the white-and-yellow envelope and removed the book.

For the next few weeks, I devoured all the book’s pertinent information, and I used every waking moment to prepare my twelve portfolio pieces for review. I worked on various pieces, from charcoal drawings to hand-painted illustrations. I tried to show a broad range of abilities and interests in a condensed timeline.

I had only a month to get ready. But unfortunately, I did not come from a family of artists, and no one knew how best to support me in this part of the journey. So I stayed after school each day to work alongside Lasar in the art studio. I felt uncomfortable being alone and often tried to find other students to ask for help.

I wished I had Mr. Summers by my side.

Much to my surprise, my new art teacher was cruel and unwelcoming. She believed I did not have the requisite skills to get into such a prestigious school.

"What are you doing?" she asked every time I entered the studio.

"I'm working on my portfolio for CCS," I replied, walking straight toward the back of the classroom to avoid further interactions.

"CCS? Really? Kids like you don't end up at CCS. You end up dead or in jail." Her words were consistently dismissive and infuriating.

I struggled to complete all of the required pieces of artwork in her classroom after school. But, once again, I felt determined to prove her words did not break me. I knew in my heart my dreams were valid and my aspirations would come true.

After four weeks of grinding, I was ready to submit my portfolio and forgo my desire to pursue mechanical and electrical engineering.

With my parents' assistance, I filled out the application, gathered all of the critical requirements, and rushed to the post office to send out my portfolio before the deadline at midnight. I had prepared to the best of my ability and was determined to achieve my newfound goal of becoming an industrial designer.

A month passed, and CCS notified us my work was considered fit for admission, but they required an in-person interview to determine if I had the skill and work ethic to be a CCS student.

My parents were elated by the news. Despite their limited understanding of my passion, they gave me unwavering support and encouragement. We collectively decided which date would work best for our road trip to Detroit and subsequently made arrangements for our adventure.

We set out with the intention of coming home with good news.

We had never been to Detroit as a family, so we felt confident that despite our lack of knowledge of the city, our preparation and resolve would provide us with everything we needed to endure.

God was the architect of this moment, and faith forged the foundation of our conviction.

When we arrived in Detroit, its expansive yet decrepit downtown shocked my mother.

"Ugh . . . we worked way too hard for him to be dropped right back off in the hood," she said to my father as we drove down Woodward Avenue, staring at the vacant high-rise buildings, burned-down homes, and empty blocks.

The city's post-apocalyptic essence would worry any concerned mother if they were asked to leave their child unattended in what appeared to be a city frozen in despair.

However, I saw familiarity—a reflection of why I was striving to do the impossible. I was young, hungry, and determined. Nothing would stop me, not even my own parents' fears. Detroit was where I belonged.

After an hour of touring the city, we finally arrived at CCS. The landscape encapsulated the modern architectural styles of iconoclasts such as William Kessler and Minoru Yamasaki. Their bold visions shaped the look and feel of the campus. The buildings exuded the hard-earned confidence of a city that gave birth to revolutionaries and industrialists.

We approached the admissions office to check in. Again, my parents reaffirmed my desire to gain admittance and encouraged me to advocate for myself with complete confidence and certainty that I was as good as any student walking through the door that day. Their words were the reminder I needed.

"What is meant for you is for you, Jason. God did not bring us this far to leave us here."

We ascended the stairs, entered the office, and sat; my hands trembled. I was sitting in the presence of my destiny. I knew my curiosity and work ethic had led me to this moment.

I sat, silent, prepared to give my all.

Sabrina Nelson, a proud, intelligent Black woman, would be my interviewer that day. She had a heart for students from schools where CCS had not recruited anyone. She told me about her family, her love for Chicago, and how difficult CCS and its intense workload were.

While we spoke, a panel of professors from various departments reviewed my work and determined my future. I was nervous but unshakable in my spirit. I knew I belonged.

As they emerged with their final decision, Sabrina's facial expression changed from joy to concern. Was it bad news? Did I not get accepted? What did I do wrong?

"Well, I have some good news and not-so-good news."

She explained they had determined my portfolio to be exceptional considering my limited experience; however, it needed to be more robust for an industrial design applicant to gain admittance successfully. So, instead, they recommended I major in graphic design or illustration.

The news devastated me.

I had come all this way only to have a panel of strangers tell me they alone had the sovereign authority to assess my gifts.

I rebelled against this outcome and remembered what my parents had told me: "Advocate for your dreams, son. Do not take no for an answer."

I closed my eyes, inhaled peace, exhaled hesitation, and spoke.

"I understand they may feel I am not good enough for ID. That's fine. I'm not here to prove them wrong; I'm here to prove God right. God gave me a vision of what my life could be with effort and focus. I refuse to believe it cannot come true. How about this? Why don't you let me into ID? And if I fail, I will gladly switch to graphic design or illustration. How does that sound?"

Sabrina was stunned. A student had never put her in a situation where she had to negotiate. I had no plan B. I had no safety net. I was all in for my dream and determined to leave as an ID student.

She arose, excused herself momentarily, and took my counteroffer back to the committee. As time passed, I sat and prepared for the worst. Despite my outward calm, I was extremely nervous. Finally, after what felt like a lifetime, she returned.

This time her energy was infectious, her smile celebratory and supportive.

"I have good news. You can come as an ID student, *but* you will need to start on probation. So if you fail, it would be easier for you to immediately switch to a new major. You have to earn it, but based on what you showed me just now, I do not have any doubts about you, brother. You have a gift, and you clearly will not leave here without a *yes*. Welcome to CCS."

One step closer to my dream, I rushed out of the office, ran to my parents, and fell into my mother's arms. I cried tears of joy. All my years of searching and seeking had come to an end.

I was one step closer to finding my way to Nike.

CHAPTER 6

ARE YOU THE INTERN?

When opportunity meets preparation, remarkable things occur.

Upon returning from Detroit, my last few months of high school were a blur. But after graduation, every day I reread the prospective student handbook I received from College for Creative Studies.

I stared for hours at the marker rendering of a Ford GT on the front cover. I could not wait to learn how to create at that level. So, as the summer came to a close, we packed my belongings, arranged a family caravan from Chicago to Detroit, and embarked on an adventure together.

My first year at CCS was incredibly humbling. I was not as prepared as my peers; however, what I lacked in talent, I made up for in my work ethic. My professors took notice of the volume of work I produced. My willingness to go above and beyond the required ask for each assignment slowly gained their respect. Each quarter I tried to find a way to show I wanted to compete with the best despite my limited skill set.

As the year progressed, I climbed from the bottom of the class to securely above the median student's grade point average and safely secured my second-year spot in industrial design.

I had made the cut, barely. Despite a rejection for a Nike internship that year, my confidence soared. I was unaware I needed to be in my junior year to successfully obtain a coveted Adrenaline Internship position. I was disappointed but not dismayed.

That summer, I returned home and vowed to apply my athletic mindset to design.

For designers, that translates to proper sketching technique earned through muscle memory.

"Draw from your shoulder," my teachers would tell me when I sketched products. This verbal prompt reminded me to use my arm as a fluid hinge. I focused on keeping my hand, wrist, and elbow aligned as I gracefully sketched without curling my wrist.

Concept artists, illustrators, and designers use this technique to improve the quality of their sketch lines. The goal was to control the line quality by effortlessly transitioning from thick to thin lines, creating shape and dimension along the way.

I decided to give myself a training regimen consisting of weekly trips to the Art Institute of Chicago, figure drawing courses, art history lessons, and one thousand doodles daily.

I would fill up notebooks and draw on napkins, newspapers, and more. Wherever there was a pen and paper, I would practice. I knew if I wanted to be the best, I needed to outwork my insecurity.

This routine lasted for two summers. I worked as a janitor and mover four days a week and attended art classes two days a week. After the first summer, I returned to CCS and rose to the top 1 percent of my class. After applying for a Nike internship in my sophomore year, I received a rejection email from Nike stating, "Thank you for submitting your portfolio. Unfortunately, you were not selected for this year's Adrenaline Program, but please try again next year."

Each submission and subsequent rejection was strategic. I wanted Nike's recruiters to be familiar with my name, and I wanted them to witness my growth and development as a design student.

My junior year finally arrived, and I had worked my way to the top for over two years. I was the best student in industrial design at CCS and one of the top students in the country. In addition, I competed in and won several sponsored design competitions for illustrious prizes, including a chance to study abroad in France while working as a designer for Renault. Naturally, I felt proud of my accomplishments, but nothing compared to the illusive feeling of finally receiving an opportunity from Nike.

After receiving the news from my professors about the chance to live and work in Paris, I was strangely sad and conflicted.

Compared to other opportunities, working for Renault and attending Strate School of Design would be a life-changing experience for me as a Black man. I would be immersed in another culture and language while surrounded by like-minded creatives from all corners of the world.

As the winter quarter came to a close, our department chair, Professor Clyde Foles, called me into his office.

"Hey, Jason. When you return from break, let us know if you're going or staying. It's up to you, son. Do what works best for your future and your career."

I rose, shook his hand, and walked out the door without saying a word. My heart raced as I pondered the outcome of my decisions.

As I walked across campus back to my dorm, I thought, *If I turn this down and Nike doesn't come through, I would be blowing a tremendous opportunity.*

Despite the magnitude of the choice I had to make, I persisted. In my heart, I knew if this was my final chance at being accepted into Nike's Adrenaline Program, a preeminent summer internship for college athletes and elite students, I needed to wait. Paris would not be my next chapter.

I packed my bags and instructed my roommate, a reclusive freshman from rural Michigan named Jeremiah, not to answer the phone during winter break and to let all calls go to voice mail. I was a newly appointed resident assistant, and at the time, I did not own a cell phone, and he was the only person I could rely on, although he had a peculiar personality.

During the first part of the year, we barely spoke. Jeremiah spent most of his time on the floor of our apartment, building a scaled Lego replica of our nation's capital. So I had concerns with his ability to capture the call's details accurately should Nike reach out to notify me of my acceptance.

"Hey, J, you have a second?"

"Yep," he replied, barely lifting his head to acknowledge my question.

"Listen, I'm taking off for the break in a few minutes, but before I dip, I ask that you let all calls go to voice mail. You have a cell phone, and you're from Michigan, so you can connect with your family anytime over break. I still need to get a phone, and the only number Nike has is this one. I may come back earlier, so I told them to call and leave a message, just in case. So please, do not answer the phone. It's important. Cool?"

His response to my passionate plea was a simple, "Okay."

The tone of his underwhelming response let me know that he indeed would drop the ball. So I closed my eyes, prayed, and slowly walked out the door.

Days later, Jeremiah would confirm my suspicion. Lisa Olivia, Nike's design recruiter at the time, would indeed call, and my roommate decided to answer the phone despite my firm instructions.

"Can I speak to Jason Mayden? This is Lisa from Nike. I wanted to give him some good news."

"Yeah. What's up?" Jeremiah replied.

"Jason! Congratulations! Welcome to the Adrenaline Program. We are so excited to have you *finally* join us. We have been cheering you on all of these years, and we are impressed with your growth."

At this moment, any relatively mature human being would interject and inform the other party that they were not the intended recipient of the message. Not my roommate—he was different.

Distracted by a sea of Legos and a bowlful of unseasoned shrimp, he muttered, "Okay, thanks," and hung up.

Something about the interaction with my roommate must have triggered her intuition. She called back, this time leaving a message that provided me with her contact information and a clarifying story about why she needed to ensure the person she spoke to was indeed me.

At the end of each break, resident assistants customarily arrived a week before their residents. The students who occupied the dorm over the holiday were typically international students or people who opted to stay in Detroit over the break.

As I returned from Christmas break, I anxiously rode the elevator to the fifth floor. Then, finally, the doors opened, and my residents that stayed over the break met me at the door with a sea of orange balloons.

I had not heard anything from my roommate, so I did not assume the balloons were related to my Nike internship, despite the color being similar to Nike's classic shoebox. It was an art school, and art kids were spontaneous and weird. I commonly saw things like that all over campus. Public displays of self-expression were typical.

I approached my dorm room door, opened it carefully to ensure I did not wake my roommate, and before I could place my bags on the floor, my resident and friend Skip opened his door, rushed over the threshold of my room, and yelled, *"Dude, you're f——g going to Nike!"*

His words did not register immediately.

"Huh? What are you talking about? No one ever called me, and I told Jeremiah not to answer the phone, so what are you talking about?"

"He didn't tell you? Lisa from Nike called. You got the internship. She left a message."

I was overcome with joy and rage simultaneously. I was astounded Jeremiah did not notify me of the message, let alone the conversation I instructed him *not* to have numerous times before the break.

As my anger rose, my roommate sheepishly peered out of the kitchen with his latest batch of shrimp and said in a monotone voice, "Oh, yeah. Nike called. You got the internship."

I abandoned my composure, dropped my bags, squared my stance, and lunged at the Lego sculpture, punting the Capitol building against the wall. Then, as the Legos poetically ruptured, ricocheting off the ceiling and falling to the ground like confetti, I turned and ran to the answering machine to hear the message from my future employer.

The forty-five seconds it took to listen to the message felt like a lifetime.

"Hi, it's me again, Lisa; not sure if I spoke to Jason or not. I was hoping for a more exciting response, considering this is your dream. If the person I spoke with was not Jason, can you please have him call me back when he has a moment? Thank you. Talk soon. Bye."

I immediately called Lisa, hoping to apologize and clear up the confusion my roommate caused. Thankfully, her instincts were correct. We shared a laugh, and she encouraged me to enjoy the moment.

"Take a second and let it all sink in. You did it. Welcome to Nike."

It was finally happening. I had arrived at the place I dreamed about each night. Above my bed on the ceiling, I had placed an image of Nike's campus. It was the first thing I saw when I woke up and the last thing I saw when I went to sleep. Now I would be a part of that image. I would add to the magic and majesty of a company that inspired a generation of kids to dream big.

I would finally belong.

As the second half of the school year progressed, the news of my accomplishment spread among the students, faculty, and administration.

I had gone from the kid admitted to CCS on artistic probation to the top student of my class. I had achieved the impossible outcome many deemed unrealistic. I was going to Nike.

The Black and Latino students and staff took time to celebrate my journey. The janitors and security guards who brought me food and words of wisdom during my numerous all-nighters were equally proud of what I had done.

They held me down when no one believed I could do it. They served as a proxy for my family's elders, often providing me with a warm smile and an encouraging word from God. I would carry them all with me on my adventure. They had become my tribe.

I shared the news with Professor Foles and informed him of my decision to pursue Nike over Renault. Now I had to finish the year successfully and proceed to Beaverton, Oregon. I was ahead on schoolwork; I finally had enough money to purchase a cell phone and successfully secured my summer work plans.

What could go wrong?

Several weeks before the beginning of summer break, I unexpectedly received a call from a 503 area code while watching a movie with my classmates.

Days prior, I had given Nike my new phone number, so I assumed the call was about incomplete paperwork or an impromptu introduction.

I reached into my jacket pocket, retrieved my T-Mobile Sidekick, and answered, "Hello, Jason Mayden speaking."

People in Detroit always answered their phones in the movie theater, so I did not feel awkward opening my flip phone and responding with an enthusiastic tone.

"Hey, Jason, this is Dave from Nike. I'm also a CCS alum. So good to meet you! Hey, I have some good news, and I have some bad news."

Uh oh. I thought. I had heard that phrase before, years prior, during the CCS portfolio review process.

"What up, Dave? Great to meet you. What's the bad news?" I asked, bracing for the worst.

"Well, first, this has nothing to do with you or your talent, but Nike Basketball lost its budget for their intern. However, are you interested in a new role? Jordan Brand is interested in having you as their first intern. What do you think? Can that work?"

I stood in shock, abruptly ejecting the large popcorn bucket in my lap into the air and onto the row in front of me. "*Yes*!" I rushed out of the theater and into the hall to finish the call.

My classmates laughed as the movie theater audience slowly exited, unsure of my mental state. I didn't care if they thought I was crazy. I was going to Nike as Jordan Brand's first design intern, *and* I was one step closer to becoming the real-life Dr. Lucius Fox.

The brand founded and inspired by my hero, Michael Jordan, would become the first stop on my professional journey.

Dave erupted in laughter. He knew I would be elated, and his message delivery was sneakily deceptive. "Congrats, dude. I know how bad you wanted this. It showed in your work. It's bada——s." He continued, "Over the next few months, a few people will reach out to give you more information so you are ready to rock this summer. In the meantime, finish strong and reach out if you need anything. I got you."

I was all set. I had accomplished my goal.

Over the next few months, I received onboarding documents, roommate assignments, and my manager's contact info in anticipation of my arrival at Nike's campus in June.

On our scheduled arrival day, human resources staff instructed us to meet for our orientation in Steve Prefontaine Hall, the building where Phil Knight, the founder and CEO of Nike, was waiting to welcome us personally.

We were the best of the best, students and student athletes from all over the world in one room with one shared dream—to someday work at Nike. As orientation concluded, the internship coordinator instructed us to review our campus maps and proceed to our assigned building to meet our manager.

But, to my surprise, the most impactful sponsored athletes' names adorned the entrances of each building on campus. In addition, the layout and artifacts in each lobby prominently transform the Nike campus into an open-air sports museum.

I strode toward the Michael Jordan building to locate my desk and meet my team. As I entered, I approached the front desk.

"Hi, I'm Jason Mayden. I am looking for Bob Mervar. I'm an intern in Jordan."

"Um. Right athlete, wrong building." The receptionist laughed as she informed me I was in the wrong place. "Jordan is located on the fourth floor of the Jerry Rice building. Here, let me show you how to get there." She took my map, drew out the quickest route, and called ahead to inform my manager I was on my way.

As I approached the building, I felt overwhelmed with emotion. I entered the elevator, pressed the fourth-floor button, and studied the map, hoping to look like I knew where to walk once I arrived at my destination.

The door opened, and my head was still down, studying the map in great detail. Then, instantly, my gaze shifted from the map to the two men's pairs of Italian dress shoes waiting to enter the elevator to depart.

I looked up slowly, and much to my surprise, there stood Michael Jordan and Jordan Brand's president, Larry Miller.

Without hesitation, I lowered my gaze and pretended to be lost while attempting to close the door and return to the lobby.

Unfortunately, I accidentally pressed the button informing the elevator that the doors should remain open.

MJ and Larry stood there in amazement, watching me fiddle with the buttons nervously. Their presence obviously left me in a state of shock.

The door jutted open; Michael reached his hand inside the door and poked his finger into the center of my chest.

"Are you the intern?" he asked.

"Yes. Yes, sir. I'm . . . the intern."

"How did you get here?" he asked with a tone of admiration and surprise.

"Uh, I took the elevator?" I responded, unsure of the nature of his question.

Michael and Larry burst into laughter.

"No, man, how did you get *here*? To Jordan from Chicago. You must be hungry. You must really want this."

He was familiar with my neighborhood and understood the complexity of surviving in the city and the education system.

I explained my story, starting with my hospitalization at seven years old and ending with how I made it into CCS—stumbling over my words, hoping to say something that would make me memorable. As I concluded, he gently grabbed my shoulders, moved me aside, and entered the elevator to depart.

As the doors closed, I blurted out, "Do you have any advice? How can I succeed?"

In typical MJ fashion, he responded quietly, "Don't f——k up."

The door closed, and I stood there astonished, having come face-to-face with my childhood hero.

Until this day, those three words serve as the basis of how I navigate every circumstance and opportunity. What MJ imparted to me was sound wisdom. When opportunity meets preparation, one must be ready to seize the moment.

In every endeavor, I understand the value of the circumstance, my privilege, and the power of my purpose.

I hold on to his wisdom and walk with grace and empathy for others.

Because when it is all said and done, we are just grown children striving not to f——k up our God-given, hard-earned opportunities.

CHAPTER 7

THE WAITING PLACE

"Delayed" does not mean "denied."

In my life, I often heard from adults that you should never meet your heroes because they may not be who you think they are. However, in my case, meeting my hero ignited an insatiable desire to capture the beautiful bounty of confidence hidden within my moment.

The divine energy of my aspirations fueled my work ethic and allowed me to carry myself with the disposition of a tenured employee during my time as an intern at Nike.

I focused on offering solutions while other interns spent their time socializing. They did not appreciate the magnitude of the moment. Jordan's leadership team noticed my efforts and maturity. I obsessed over the nuance that resided in the bedrock of Jordan's innovative "athletic luxury" brand positioning.

From Jordan, I learned greatness is doing the small things well and consistently.

As a result, my consistency made way for a life-changing opportunity at a far sooner time than I had ever imagined. My innate understanding of youth culture, fashion, technology, and the sport of basketball allowed me to design a derivative of an Air Jordan as an intern. To my surprise, Gentry Humphrey, the footwear product director, decided to green-light my idea for the lifestyle-inspired Air Jordan XVII Mule for production before my summer adventure in Beaverton, Oregon, concluded.

I had gone pro before graduating college. The gravity of the moment delighted and perplexed me. God's steady hand in my life brought forth an unimaginable outcome.

When opportunity meets preparation, miraculous outcomes ensue.

When I returned to CCS, I was bombarded with requests to meet students who shared my passion for footwear design. So we would sit in my dorm and discuss the process of creation, how Jordan operated, and what it felt like to be a part of an iconic American brand.

I felt a sense of pride and responsibility. I was now the example I wished I had when my search began.

Fully prepared for my newfound responsibilities, I immediately pursued positions on campus that would allow me to amplify the voices of those who felt unseen by the administration.

I was nominated and elected as president of our student union and our Black student union, affectionately known as BART, Black Artist Researching Trends. I inserted myself as a student advocate in budgetary discussions and academic disputes. In addition, I began to use my voice to advocate for the betterment of the collective community.

By accepting the responsibility of my influence, I gained confidence while deepening my conviction to pursue my dreams. During each interaction with Nike's recruiters, I kept them abreast of my development as a designer and student advocate. Additionally, I provided them feedback about the recruitment process, solutions to inefficiencies I experienced during my time as an intern, and ways to increase diversity in the pipeline by sponsoring courses at CCS.

As the year ended, my peers and professors celebrated my efforts, and I was given an IDSA (Industrial Designers Society of America) Student Merit Award in Design Excellence. Shortly after, I received formal interview requests from Reebok and Nike.

I was now at the precipice of my next mountain to climb.

THE WAITING CONTINUES

Over the next few months, I spent time in Beaverton and Boston, meeting with various design executives, teams, and recruiters. Countless hours of mock interviews had prepared me to speak with ease and clarity when asked why design was my career path of choice.

Themes of failure, rejection, and seeking my purpose complemented personal tales of love, sacrifice, and faith. I celebrated my family, community, trauma, and triumph with each word.

I did not feel I was there to prove anyone wrong. God only sent me to prove him right.

Jeremiah 29:11 states in the New International Version, "'For I know the plans I have for you,' declares the Lord, 'plans to prosper you and not to harm you, plans to give you hope and a future.'"

Finally, I discovered God's "plan" for my life at the intersection of design and advocacy. I was operating within my purpose, and all things were in harmony.

Despite my internship, Nike did not show me favor over other candidates. I had to wait for the outcome of the hiring panel like everyone else.

Reebok's reaction to my portfolio and interview was markedly different. They were eager and excited I had brought a different perspective to their candidate pool. After the first interview, the recruiter notified me of their intention to offer me a full-time position before I graduated a few months later. During my interview, they fell in love with my advanced knowledge of technology and my adjacency to youth culture. After I departed from Boston, they offered me a full-time, entry-level position as a designer, working on the newly announced sport luxury offering, RBK Diamond Collection.

Their binding offer and Nike's delayed response left me conflicted.

Days turned to weeks, and I was still waiting to receive an answer from my dream company. So I was once again in the waiting place.

During that period, my imagination persuaded my emotions to cloud my thoughts with anxiety.

My mind raced. Ideas of the worst possible outcomes arose while I simultaneously spoke words of affirmation to myself as a display of my faith in God.

I was a mess.

My typical traits ranged from sadness and worry to delight and confidence.

Something needed to change.

After two weeks, I could no longer stall. The time had come for me to accept Reebok's offer, and I was still waiting for word from Nike. I had decided to take the role and acquire the skills needed to return to the Swoosh one day.

Weeks later, I traveled to Boston to make it official.

On the morning of my in-person orientation at Reebok, I received an unexpected call from Tracy Teague, a design executive from Nike, who informed me they had been working on an experimental rotational program for multidisciplinary designers called "The Bench."

He apologized profusely for the lack of communication and asked if it was too late for Nike to present their offer to me.

I needed clarification.

At six in the morning, a miracle occurred as I sat in my hotel room, preparing for Reebok's daylong orientation.

Tracy called to share the good news and to offer me an opportunity to join the company of my dreams.

I was torn between honoring my commitments and pursuing my childhood aspirations.

After he disclosed the offer's details, I took a deep breath, closed my eyes, and said, "Yes. I would love to join!"

"Wonderful news! We are so excited to have you back!" he exclaimed.

I exhaled a long sigh of relief. I had finally made it. However, the reality of my decision would soon interrupt my moment of joy.

I accepted offers from two companies at the same time.

I was in Boston, preparing to meet my manager for the first time, and now I had to resign before officially stepping foot on Reebok's campus. So I rummaged through my bag for the printout of my itinerary, retrieved his contact information, and dialed his number.

As the phone rang, I practiced my resignation speech in my mind. "It's not you; it's me. My options have changed, so I feel it's best to pursue my true love."

I felt like I was breaking up with someone I had just met.

"Hello?"

"Hey, this is Jason Mayden. Is this Paul?"

"Hey, buddy. Excited to meet you today. What's up?"

There it was, that dreaded question. I was nervous but determined to follow through with the answer. I had to follow my heart.

"So, I truly appreciate the opportunity. However, I quit." The vision I held in my mind of delivering an eloquent explanation for my resignation was far different than the reality of the moment. I just blurted out the words with zero context.

After a brief moment of awkward silence, he laughed and responded, "Wait, are you serious?"

"Yes. Yes. I am serious. Nike just literally called and gave me an offer, and I accepted. I'm so sorry—" He interrupted me before I could finish my apology.

"No need to feel bad about pursuing your dreams, man. I don't blame you. I would have done the same thing. It sucks for Reebok, but I get it. You interned there, it's your dream, and you gotta take it. Good luck, man. I'll be cheering for you."

Feeling heard and supported brought me to my knees after the call ended. I sat in my hotel room, crying and rejoicing while scrambling to pack my bags to return to Detroit.

I felt invincible.

The next few months were a full sprint toward our senior show as we prepared for graduation.

Coursework became less critical as we wrapped up the final touches of our portfolio for the school-wide recruiting event.

While most students felt the pressure to impress cascading waves of recruiters looking for the magic in their design, I was fortunate. After accepting Nike's offer, I just had to relax and finish my work to the best of my abilities.

My job and my degree were secure—mission accomplished.

For the remainder of the semester, I only had to organize my work for the viewing pleasure of my family and future teammates at Nike, who decided to visit CCS to support me while searching for potential candidates who may not have considered Nike a possible employer.

Life was good.

As graduation approached, I discussed the timing of my move to Beaverton with Nike and my family. I would move west on June 4, 2002, the day after my mother's birthday.

I spent a couple of weeks in Chicago after graduation. I realized this would be my last time living at home with my parents, so I chose to enjoy every second.

When the moving day finally arrived, a wave of emotion overtook me. The next step in my adventure awaited me. My family watched as the movers packed my belongings. At the same time, I loaded my parents' car with my luggage and personal artifacts that I wanted to carry with me as I stepped into the autonomy of young adulthood. My travel, living arrangements, and schedule details were provided as part of my formal offer packet. Finally, I took flight.

I realize now that children often dream of fantastical career paths to lead them to fame and glory. Some children dream of service and finding ways to improve and protect the world around them. Others aspire to be next to their heroes as collaborators and teammates.

However, only a tiny fraction of children achieve their dreams. It is a surreal experience. Looking backward allows you to see the interdependencies of each disparate experience along your life's journey. Each inflection point adds to the tapestry of your precious memories.

In my divine quest, I had become the Black Odysseus. My adventure had taken me from the south side of Chicago to the southwest suburbs of Portland. Finally, God's grand design brought me to the end of my origin story.

I was writing a new chapter of my life in real time, and I was the protagonist. I had abandoned fear for hope. Despite my childhood setbacks, I successfully overcame my guilt and shame.

The power of my words breathed life into my ideas.

All things were in perfect harmony. Blessings arrived when I ultimately submitted to the vision God placed in my heart. I shattered the expectation and limitations assigned to me at birth by a system that often categorizes Black children with audacious dreams as "unreasonable." Unreasonable people challenge convention and change the world.

By getting to Nike, I proved anything was possible, especially for an audacious, unreasonable, neurodivergent Black kid from the south side of the Chi.

The vision of my adult life was becoming apparent. I had finally broken free of the waiting place, and I had fallen deeply in love with the process of becoming. Setbacks, failures, and disappointments were natural parts of my bold endeavor.

But as I came to understand, *delayed* indeed did not mean *denied*.

My ascension from an energetic intern to a full-time employee resulted from my determination to take an uncharted path. When my peers focused on socializing, I focused on improving my sketch quality, seeking guidance from professionals in the field, and pushing myself beyond my comfort zone by auditing finance, biomechanics, and philosophy courses.

I manifested a life I had only once dreamed of by speaking my opportunity into existence.

My words had become my reality.

CHAPTER 8

THE BENCH

If you stay ready, you don't have to get ready.

This valuable insight prepared my heart for any outcome, change in priority, or ambiguous assignment that awaited me upon my return to Oregon, the home of Nike.

Before my internship, Oregon only existed in my mind as an elementary school video game entitled *The Oregon Trail*. The game stressed the importance of owning cattle, the barter system, and how dysentery affects the health of a community traveling the country in a caravan of covered wagons. Unfortunately, despite its amusing eight-bit graphics, it did not prepare me to be a full-time resident of the Pacific Northwest and a full-fledged designer at Nike.

On my official first day back on campus, the Cross Training team selected me for my initial assignment from a rotational program for multi-hyphenate creatives entitled "The Bench." The category was the brainchild of legendary Nike designer Tinker Hatfield whose workouts at a local YMCA inspired him to invent the original footwear and apparel that established the market segment (Hatfield 2014).

The athletes that represented Cross Training were icons of Black and sports culture. Bo Jackson, Deion Sanders, Bruce Smith, Dan O'Brien, and Ken Griffey Jr. defined a generation at the intersection of human potential and exponential swag. Their effortless versatility was the athletic equivalent of 1990s hip-hop: confident, authentic, soulful, and fully expressive. I was excited to join this illustrious group of designers and innovators focused on multi-sport training and innovation.

I happily received my new assignment and proceeded to my desk, which was regarded as "reception" because of its proximity to the entrance of the design floor in the Mia Hamm building. My years of janitorial and administrative work in college allowed me to see the desk position as an opportunity to engage anyone who entered our area rather than a place of insignificance.

I was often the first person that Phil Knight, the founder of Nike, would see as he walked the halls speaking to the iconic designers who built the brand. What others saw as undesirable, I saw as divinely situated. I was physically on the path to greatness as it entered the building.

Only some people were excited for me, however. My manager took offense to my ambition and found ways to disparage me as a form of hazing. He would relentlessly criticize my abilities and laugh at my discomfort and make jokes insinuating that I affiliated with gangs due to my place of birth and style of dress.

In addition, he would ridicule me for wearing hats and oversized jerseys in a company that made its profit from selling those items to kids like me from neighborhoods like mine. The cognitive dissonance and irony in his actions were unsettling.

"What are you, a Blood or a Crip? Come on. Tell me," he would often ask. Then he would childishly slap me on the shoulder and whisper, "It's just a joke. Why do you look so angry? What, you wanna hit me? You know I can fire you and kick your a——s, right?"

This exceptionally mediocre design manager found humor in his abuse of power. He made me feel I was not successfully adding professional and cultural value to the team. Instead, he positioned my identity as being distracting and unprofessional. I felt immensely disrespected.

From my seat, I bore witness to countless guests who entered our space for executive meetings, prospective athlete signings, and critical design reviews. Each passerby revealed a new facet of Nike's culture. How we worked, how we measured success, and how we disagreed became noticeable after a while. When studying each passerby, I could detect whether or not they achieved their desired outcome in their body postures and facial expressions.

I was learning the rules of the game by simply observing the players.

Over time, everyone noticed I was sparking conversations with each visitor who passed by my small cubicle on their way to a meeting. In addition, I would strategically place artifacts, concepts, and sketches within the line of sight of all who walked by.

Creating visual indicators of my interest and aptitude captured the attention of E. Scott Morris, Design Director of Nike Football. E. Scott was a prototypical player-coach. He was a verbose Black man from the north side of Chicago with a magnetic personality that endeared anyone lucky enough to be under his tutelage.

On one fateful afternoon, E. Scott abruptly entered my area and asked if I could speak with him for a moment.

"Hey, have you heard who is coming in next week?" he asked in an animated tone.

"Naw? Who? MJ?" I responded. Only Michael Jordan could elicit such a response from a seasoned vet.

"Nope. More like Iverson, but with a football."

My eyes enlarged from disbelief.

Was Nike bringing the phenom from Virginia Tech to campus to be signed? Was Michael Vick going to be a part of the Swoosh?

I pondered why he was telling me, a new hire with less than three months of actual work experience. Immediately, I said in a confused tone, "Vick?"

"Yes, sir. Correct. Mr. M7 *himself*," he said as he clapped his hands with the force of a quarterback breaking a huddle.

"That's crazy. Why are you telling me, though?" I asked, fighting back laughter. E. Scott bounced up and down, mimicking the pregame ritual of an athlete anxiously waiting to sprint onto the field.

"He may need a logo. I'm just saying," E. Scott said as he shrugged and backpedaled away from my cube toward his next impromptu conversation.

I dissected his subliminal prompt quickly. I was encouraged to create from a place of lived experience and cultural understanding. He knew my actual value at that moment was my present connection to the raw energy of youth culture. I was a designer and a consumer of the brand. My insight was invaluable.

In my newness, I brought a sense of creative innocence not yet subjugated to the machine of corporate creativity. I was free to see the wonder in every task given to me. So I decided to take action.

Two weeks later, on the eve of Vick's visit, I critically inspected the culmination of a self-directed design sprint. I would create the branding while collaborating with my close friend and former internship roommate, Will Scott, on the brand positioning and narrative. We made a pact to return to Nike as a unit the year before.

His time at Florida A&M University, a prestigious historically Black college, taught him how to navigate corporate America while maintaining a firm sense of identity and resolve. Like me, he was unapologetically Black and determined to make an impact. Alone we were strong; together we were unstoppable.

So, with everything in divine order, Will was assigned to Nike's football brand marketing function. He had also been notified of Michael Vick's pending visit and had positioned himself as the most qualified candidate to support the man's brand-building efforts. As a former two-sport collegiate student athlete, he understood the depths of Vick's power and potential.

The outcome was magnificent—a full vision with context and meaning. I returned to campus later that evening to print an oversized, high-resolution image of Vick's logo. For our presentations, we often mounted our designs on large-scale foam boards for visibility and appeal; I had decided this method would be the easiest way to engage Vick directly without saying one word.

I spray-mounted the image, rushed to my desk, and leaned the board against my cubicle's back wall to ensure my design was concealed from public view.

Then, as night turned to dawn, I rushed to the employee gym, named after prolific multi-sport icon Bo Jackson, to shower and change clothes before the convoy of sports agents, entourage, Nike executives, and Vick arrived from his campus tour in the morning.

I returned to my desk, flipped the board over, and sat patiently, pretending to be in deep focus as I sketched footwear concepts for an entry-level assignment, the Nike Air Monarch II.

The project had no budget, athlete, or advanced innovation, but I took the assignment seriously despite its lack of appeal. Much like the MV7 logo, I realized that finding joy in a small task meant I had the maturity and discipline required to take on higher-profile projects. So, despite having a looming deadline to present the Monarch II to Phil Knight and Nike Design leadership, I was determined to finish the logo to show the breadth and depth of my abilities.

When the moment finally arrived, I displayed my interpretation of Vick's athletic disposition in the form of a 3D-modeled crest rendered with a brushed aluminum finish. The composition encapsulated the sharp edges of the expressive number seven within a stylized silhouette of a football that subtly contained his initials.

Upon his arrival, Vick and his convoy exited the elevator; they each stopped and gazed at the board with confusion and delight. The last people to leave the elevator were Vick and Howard "H" White, the VP of Jordan Brand Sports Marketing and the unofficial Nike and Jordan historian.

In his younger days, H was a highly recruited athlete from Virginia, the same birth state as Vick. H and I formed a close bond during my internship. He positioned himself as a mentor, pastor, and surrogate uncle for young Black interns who had all found a home in his office, sitting on the couch while he spoke life over our dreams.

"JayMay. What's good? I wanna introduce you to somebody." H spotted me at my desk and gravitated toward the board, conveniently positioned in his direct line of sight.

"What's up, H? How you doing, man?" I replied in a calm tone, hoping to hide my nervousness as he examined the board with the gaze of a proud coach.

"I'm mighty fine. Mighty fine, JayMay. Hey, you may know this guy here; Vick, get on over here. Let me introduce you to JayMay. He was our first design intern last year, and he's from the south side of Chicago. He's a bad man. Great designer. Y'all should meet."

Acknowledging my work, H positioned me as part of the effort to recruit Vick. He used his position of influence to create an opportunity for me. He was paying it forward in real time. He had a reputation for being the type of leader we now describe as having a high EQ and IQ. He paid close attention to how he spoke. His words created life within the hearts of all fortunate enough to be in his presence. At this moment, he directed his focus and effort toward me.

"What's up, man? Nice to meet you. What's this? This cold?" Vick asked with a tone of confident curiosity. He knew the answer but wanted to hear me say it.

"Ah, man, this? This is for you. I heard you were coming in, and I decided to play around with an idea for your logo. I didn't expect you to see it, though," I said with a hint of irony hidden in my tone.

"Stop playing; this thing is d——n near ten feet tall," Vick replied. The three of us erupted into laughter as H ushered me into the room to join the convoy.

"Grab the board and come on," he said.

Patiently, I sat in the back of the room until my time came to share a bit more about the icon and its meaning. I shared how Vick's speed, agility, and crossover appeal were unlike anything we had ever seen in football. His style and disposition instantly spoke to the youth. He was one of us.

The response was overwhelmingly positive. Vick was blown away by the detail, understanding of his desired positioning, and the boldness in my approach. Nike had provided him with an abundance of opportunity, and in that instant, he committed to signing with the Swoosh. My daring move had paid off, and I felt deep gratitude for E. Scott and H, who recognized the power to position me in a favorable light early on in my career.

I was right where I belonged.

CHAPTER 9

GAME TIME

Nothing in this life lasts forever—not even your problems.

We all face defining moments in our lives. Tragedy and triumph are precise indicators of our progress toward achieving our wildest dreams. Sometimes, setbacks cause us to deviate from the path we hoped to follow. These deviations are sometimes God's way of putting us into the appropriate position to receive a blessing from an unlikely circumstance.

The ambiguity of the unknown can get us closer to our destiny.

My brave display of confidence caused my manager to increase his hazing. Moreover, the news of Michael Vick's adoption of my logo exacerbated his entitled attitude. He believed I did not deserve the esteem that came with such an impressive outcome.

"What are you, a p——y? Why can't you take a joke? It's part of our culture. But c'mon, man, you need to relax."

My manager used these familiar taunts to try and interrupt my peace. His weapon of choice was his sharp-tongued, demeaning comments masked as wisecracks. Instead of engaging in verbal combat, I often removed myself from the situation, reached out to other Black employees, and left Nike's campus to breathe and recenter myself before returning to my desk.

One of the employees I reached out to was Josiah Lake, a former Nike intern, collegiate athlete, and full-time product line manager of Jordan Brand. He considered himself a native of Oregon by way of Tennessee. His unique upbringing and cultural identity existed at the intersection of two vastly different Black realities.

His Tennessee roots forged one reality in the fire of Southern pride and prejudice and the other in the heart of an American experiment that became the state of Oregon.

His cultural agility allowed him to understand how to deal with the normal Oregon passive aggressiveness and micro-aggressions. When things became progressively worse for me at work, I endured by asking Josiah to lunch to discuss my experiences and hopefully find an appropriate path forward.

At that time, the small community of Black employees sought refuge in one another. We created an informal yet familial network of Black professionals using an early social media website, Black Planet, to connect with other young professionals who had come west for opportunities at companies like Nike and Intel.

Our professional and personal lives merged into a singular experience. Our community served as a recreation hub and a place to receive guidance. In our group chat, I commonly saw requests like "Where is the nearest Black barber?" or "How should I handle this salary negotiation?"

We made a home among ourselves where we could be honest and vulnerable without judgment or ridicule. But we lived in a state whose Black inhabitants made up less than 1 percent of the total population. As Black employees of the Swoosh, our experience in Oregon was harrowing. Those who moved west hoping to work for a company that profited from its proximity to Black exceptionalism often felt isolated from the world.

Each moment felt surreal.

One afternoon in 2003, while sheltering from a recent barrage of verbal insults, Josiah and I ventured into Northeast Portland to buy various items to accompany us on our product development trips to Asia before winter break. Designers, developers, and product marketers customarily visited Nike's development centers in places like China, Taiwan, Korea, and Thailand before the end of our calendar year.

These trips allowed us to confirm critical samples, order materials with long lead times, and establish key priorities for the first quarter of the following year.

As Josiah and I rode to the mall, we discussed the nature of my circumstances, our future goals, our aspirations, and our desires to start families at a young age, since we had both grown up with young parents who were deeply engaged and involved in our development.

"How does it feel to be back, man?" Josiah asked as we arrived at our destination.

"To be honest, it still hasn't sunk in. I can't believe I'm here. I just want to make the most of the moment, bro. I'm not letting anyone or anything distract me. I'm married to this moment. Until God provides a better bride, this is it for me. I'm not messing this up."

Josiah burst into laughter. "I feel you, man. But you ain't married to this. You got a girl, right?"

"Nope. It's me, myself, and I."

I was not actively seeking a relationship. I had gotten into my dream job and decided to rely on God to provide me with the person he intended for me. As a result, I never put much effort into maintaining a serious relationship. Instead, I was deeply in love with the vision for my life manifesting before my eyes. We continued to walk for a few more minutes before abruptly shifting the tone of our conversation.

"Peep. We can go upstairs to Foot Locker, grab a few white tees, five for twenty dollars, and dip," Josiah said as we walked briskly from our car to the mall's main entrance.

"Cool, sounds like a plan," I replied, knowing we both had limited time before returning to campus for meetings.

We rushed up the stairs, entered Foot Locker, bought our travel gear, and descended the steps toward the garage.

At that exact moment, Josiah tapped me on the shoulder and said, "Peep, she looks like your type." With an eager grin, he jerked his head toward someone behind us.

"Man, I'm not focused on that right now. If it's meant to be, I will see her again. Portland is extremely small, bro."

I turned and noticed the woman he was referring to standing behind the jewelry store counter where she worked, engaging with a customer. She captured my attention immediately. Her thick, dark curls, radiant smile, and warm gaze drew me in as I passed. She was my type, but today was not the day to approach her. If this was indeed in God's plan, we would meet again in a natural way. I did not want to deviate from my path, nor did I want to disrupt her day at work. So, despite my interest, I decided to depart. I was placing our subsequent encounter in the hands of fate.

Meanwhile, life was becoming a series of uncomfortable indoctrinations into adulthood. However, I still needed to find an apartment that would accept my application, as my time in corporate housing was about to end.

I had run out of extensions and was too afraid to ask my parents for help. I wanted them to view me as capable of figuring things out independently. I had a voice. I knew how to advocate, but I needed to be better versed in how my lack of credit history would work against me.

I assumed my letter of employment as a designer at Nike and my check stubs would be enough to secure a safe, reasonably priced apartment.

However, I grossly miscalculated how hard it would be to find a place to live.

Over the next few weeks before our trip, I scrambled to find a stable residence before we departed for Asia. Unfortunately, the limited items I transported from Chicago to Beaverton would remain in storage, and I had to accept the reality that I would go unhoused for a short period.

I had no credit card, no credit history, and no one local to ask for help, and I thought if my manager found out I could not secure a place to live, he would use that information against me. So I hid the nature of my circumstance behind a disarming smile and did not seek additional help from Nike. My pride and embarrassment precluded me from seeking further assistance elsewhere.

In addition, I had limited savings and no wealthy family member to provide a safe harbor. Left without a choice, I transitioned my place of rest from temporary corporate housing to my car and sometimes my cubicle.

In the trunk of my loyal champagne-gold Chrysler Cirrus, I neatly stored all of my belongings alongside toiletries and basic supplies. I would often bounce around Nike's campus after hours, evading security, trying my best to maintain composure during work hours after showering and getting dressed in the locker room of the employee gym each morning.

I would use my lunch breaks to visit apartments, share my financial records, and pray someone would trust I could pay consistently for my living expenses. For three weeks, I felt the humiliation of being simultaneously employed and houseless—a feeling many people face.

I developed a profound empathy for the working poor, the struggling single parent, or the foster child who outgrew the system with no place to receive them. Despite having a large family in Chicago, I had no one to turn to except the people I did not want to disappoint the most, my teammates in Jordan.

During my internship, D'Wayne Edwards was in Nike's ACG group, but his presence and influence often worked into the Jordan Brand. Born and raised in Inglewood, California, D'Wayne was a walking example of beating the odds.

He was a self-taught Black designer who found his way to the highest levels of design when he was tasked with leading Jordan footwear design as the director at the age of thirty-one. He had begun to assemble a team while looking for ways to bring others along with him. Suzette Henri, an elegant Black woman who was a well-respected color-and-materials designer in luxury and performance, had recently joined the team.

For weeks, D'Wayne reached out to schedule a day and time to have lunch with me and the Jordan design team. He was eager to reconnect to learn how things had gone since I rejoined the company. I had travel plans, urgent meetings, or competing deadlines to use as an excuse not to meet while I looked for an apartment.

Whenever I saw D'Wayne around Nike's campus, he would ask, "What's up, lil bro? When are we going to connect?"

"Soon, bro, soon. They have me slammed in Cross Training. You know how it goes."

I hesitated to attend the meeting. I did not want to inform D'Wayne of my struggles to find housing and the micro-aggressions I was experiencing. Somehow, I believed this was my fault, and I needed to figure it out alone.

After his numerous attempts to have me visit the team for lunch, I decided communing with like-minded people who looked like me could be the oasis of hope I needed. As I entered the design area, D'Wayne dapped me up. He was wearing his typical uniform, which consisted of a crisp white T-shirt, denim pants, and boots. He introduced me to Suzette. "Hey, meet your birthday twin. Now I have to deal with *two* of y'all Libras."

She laughed and quickly responded, "D'Wayne, hush." Onlookers broke into laughter.

She greeted me with the warmth of a familiar soul. She physically looked like my mother—brown skin, wavy hair, and an electric smile. Her presence was comforting. We had begun to speak about our moves and where we currently lived.

"Where do you live, Jay?"

I hesitated to respond, which caused D'Wayne to probe with the intensity of a concerned older brother.

"Hey, lil bro, where are you living, dude?" he asked again with more significant concern.

"Right now I'm in between places. I'll be right. I have to figure it out," I said with a forced tone of certainty.

My answer did not suffice.

"I know the manager at my apartment complex. I live near D'Wayne. Would you like me to introduce you?" Suzette offered lovingly, sensing I was lying about my circumstances. "I can introduce you. Just let me know."

"That would be great. I really would appreciate that," I said, fighting back tears of relief. At that moment, I felt comfortable sharing I had difficulty finding a place to live because of my limited credit history.

She smiled. "That's all? Okay, I got you. We got you. I'll talk to her and cosign if I need to."

I barely knew Suzette, yet she offered to vouch for my financial responsibility—not because she had to but because she and D'Wayne had dedicated their lives to fighting for fairness and equity for young Black creatives, despite being young Black creatives themselves. She heard the unspoken things and leaped into action with a mother's care and concern.

Later that week, I visited the complex to view my first adult home, a five-hundred-square-foot, one-bedroom apartment with little natural light and poor acoustics. It was perfect. The experience of sleeping in my car and underneath my desk gave me a grateful heart.

The manager informed me she was hesitant to give me the apartment; however, Suzette's advocation and honesty compelled her to give me a chance. I needed to put down a larger deposit, and the place would be mine. Things were finally taking a turn for the better.

"Thank you for this. I never had anything in my name—no clue about how to rent anything other than a movie from Blockbuster video. I truly appreciate this. Thank you!" I said. Then, I departed to make it back to Nike in time for my next meeting.

Now that I had found a place to live, I could shift my focus toward my family in Chicago. I just needed to wait for the current tenant to vacate the apartment in a few days, and it would be all mine. The next day, I returned to the same mall where I bought my shirts not long ago to buy a graduation gift for my older brother.

He had decided to attend college part-time while he worked to invest more time in his dream of becoming a music producer. I was torn between purchasing him a watch or cash inside a sentimental card. The timepiece symbolized his achievement, but the money could be invested in his dream.

I entered the mall and walked directly into the jewelry store to discover the woman Josiah pointed out was again back at work, greeting customers as they entered. I smiled and walked over to her coworker to avoid interacting with her directly. I shared that I was looking for a gift for my brother, and I was particular about the weight of the watch. I wanted something to feel valuable and substantial. As a Nike designer, I was careful about finding a timepiece with what I deemed the "right" weight.

After discussing the details of my question, she abruptly excused herself to retrieve the scale from the back room. To my surprise, she returned with her coworker, Sonny, the woman I had noticed months earlier. She stood right in front of me. Fate had indeed allowed our paths to cross once again.

"Would you please mind weighing these watches for me?" I asked with a nervous grin. Her energy and alluring eyes had caught my attention, and I could not appear disinterested. We discussed our backgrounds as she gathered different options for my consideration. Finally, she revealed she was in school and only worked limited weekly hours. The unlikely probability of my being there during her shift compelled me to engage further.

She laughed. "Sure. Never has anyone asked me to weigh a watch before." She wrote down the weight.

I asked, "Would you also mind writing down your number?"

"Hmm, no, I'm sorry. I don't give out my number at work," she replied with a kind smile.

"Okay, no means no. That's cool." Despite the rejection, I refused to make her feel attacked for protecting her peace. My parents raised us to respect a woman and her boundaries. My response was different from what she had experienced in the past. Men often approached her in the mall and typically cursed at her or dismissed her when she refused to acknowledge their advances.

She hesitated, disarmed by my respect. "Why should I trust you?" she replied.

"Well, if you can move to Atlanta and not know anyone, you can have dinner with someone you don't know in a city where you know everyone." During our discussion, she disclosed that she wanted to move to Atlanta to pursue her master's in psychology. I was hopeful she would find meaning in my logical response.

"Okay, fair enough. I'll give you my number, but I am not looking for a relationship. We can go to dinner, and maybe we can be friends."

I gladly accepted her terms as I gathered the information for the watches. I needed to return to work, but our encounter lingered in my mind for the rest of the day.

The next evening, I called Sonny's number, and we spoke for hours. At our call's conclusion, we arranged to have dinner that Friday. When the day finally arrived, I picked her up from her apartment, greeted her with a bouquet, walked her to my car, and proceeded to the passenger side door. Our date felt like a reunion of kindred spirits; we shared stories of our upbringing, aspirations, and cultural similarities. She disclosed that her full name was Sonrisa, which meant *smile* in Spanish, and she had grown up between southern Oregon and Colombia. I shared details of my parents, how they had fallen in love as teenagers, my siblings 'stories, and how I ended up at Nike. Despite growing up in Oregon, she was unaware that Nike's corporate campus was minutes from where we sat.

I did not want the night to end, but I had no place to go. The current tenant of the apartment had extended their stay for an additional week. My only option was to return to Nike's headquarters for a romantic evening stroll through campus, ending with a visit to my cubicle, which also doubled as my temporary residence.

"Wow. Did you see these sketches? I had no clue Nike was here. I just thought you worked at the store. Still can't believe Nike is here in Oregon."

I burst into laughter as it became apparent that a part of her had doubted I was indeed a designer at Nike.

"It's wild, right? I still trip out too. I can't believe I really made it here. I can't believe I'm really a Nike designer."

My talent, the campus, and our instant connection blew her away. We both felt a pull toward one another. Despite our hesitation to sever our ties with independence, we would spend every moment of the next few weeks together.

We grew closer, and she became an integral part of my well-being. She was there weeks later when I welcomed my parents to my apartment. She was the first person I called when I found out my manager was moving me to Jordan. I refused to accept his ridicule, and he could not tolerate my indomitable spirit.

"We are sending you back to Jordan. It's more urban, and you will be comfortable there. It's obvious you don't understand white people." His dismissive explanation attempted to break my soul.

The sheer nature of his comments stunned me. He spoke as if he knew Nike would protect his role at all costs, and I was simply a casualty of his poor leadership.

God orchestrated a tremendous next step for me despite my manager's attempts to derail my destiny.

I was back in Jordan before I felt ready to return. The conditions of my transfer could have been more specific and straightforward, but I did not want to question God's timing.

Was a manager dedicated to my demise pushing me out? Or was God pushing me *into position*?

I chose to see it as the latter.

I had found love.

I had found peace.

I would find success.

And honestly, when the first shoe I designed in Cross Training, the Monarch, launched several months later, it became one of the most successful footwear franchises in the industry's history. Eventually, it was dubbed "the ultimate dad shoe" due to its cult following of middle-aged men. I proved my manager wrong while simultaneously shifting in the organization to live my dream sooner than I anticipated.

The reasons for my transfer to Jordan Brand may have been unclear, but I believed this was a divine intervention.

Jordan Brand called me off the bench and into the game as a starter. It was my time to shine.

CHAPTER 10

RISE OF THE JUMPMAN

I'd rather be the first me than the next anyone else.

A familiar story is shared among Black designers who joined Nike in the late 1990s and early 2000s. It is a story of a man who created an entire movement with one decision. His ancestral leaning toward adventure and belief in *the self* compelled him to make this decision.

Wilson Smith III embodied and exuded the spirit of *creatio ex nihilo* or "create from nothing" when he decided to leave a career in architecture to join what was then an unproven footwear company in Beaverton, Oregon. With this divinely inspired decision, Wilson became one of Nike's first Black designers in 1983 (Carr 2021).

I was only twenty-two when I left Nike Cross Training, after successfully designing the Monarch and the M7 logo for Michael Vick, to return to where my career began.

I had hoped to work my way up the ladder and eventually return as a senior designer to work on the Air Jordan, a dream I had carried with me since I was a little boy on the south side of Chicago.

However, as fate would have it, Wilson decided to lay out a plan based on faith and conviction. He was on his way to lead Nike Tennis and their newly formed relationship with Serena Williams. On his way out, he emphatically advocated for me to occupy his seat at the Jordan design table.

In his most sincere tone, he had asked Jordan's leadership to ensure I would be the one to replace him. After discussing this with Larry Miller, the president of Jordan Brand, he called my phone to share his intentions.

"Hey, JayMay. It's Wilson. Do you have a second? I wanted to share with you a discussion I had with Larry."

"Yep. What's up?" I replied.

"Well, I'm sure you heard about me going to Tennis, and I wanted you to know I told Larry I will only leave if you are the person who takes my spot. You deserve it. It's your dream to be here, and I feel God has allowed me to share this opportunity with you. Is that okay? I don't want to assume that—"

I abruptly interrupted Wilson mid-sentence. "Yeah. Absolutely, big bro. This is insane. Are you sure? For real? Like for real, for real? You want me to backfill you in Jordan?"

My excitement leaped through the phone as Wilson tried to contain his laughter. His gracious act of leadership allowed me to live my childhood dream.

He had heard rumblings of my experiences in Cross Training and decided to sacrifice his position to give me a chance to fulfill my heart's desire. In addition, he provided me a soft place to land when a toxic and belittling manager had reduced me to an insignificant pawn in a political display of power.

At that time, there was an immense amount of chatter regarding the future of Jordan Brand. Tinker Hatfield, the legendary Nike designer, had fully transitioned to the Innovation Kitchen. MJ had returned from retirement for the second time as a player and owner of the Washington Wizards. The confidence in his ability to transcend basketball culture had begun to fade, and the present reality of his impending retreat from the spotlight loomed over the future of the burgeoning business unit.

With younger, more relevant athletes entering the public discourse, there was a critical decision to be made. Would Jordan Brand perish under the weight of Michael Jordan's mythical ascension to the top of pop culture, or would we be able to translate the man's characteristics, ideas, and ethos into the brand? This fundamental question shaped the early strategy of Jordan Brand and how we approached identifying, grooming, and advancing talent.

As part of my onboarding, I was invited to New York in early September 2003 to shadow Wilson and Gentry Humphrey, head of Jordan footwear, as they began communicating with key retail partners, athletes, and affiliates. I would replace Wilson and eventually carry the torch for the signature products he had led over the years.

I was nervous.

My entire life had been a series of events propelling me forward to this moment. I was officially the first designer from

Chicago to be a part of Michael's legacy. Finally, *finally*, all of my childhood dreams were coming true.

I arrived in New York alone and full of angst. Who was I meeting? What should I prepare? Was I ready for this responsibility? The mixture of nervousness and childlike elation had prevented me from sleeping the entire flight. As I rode from John F. Kennedy Airport to my hotel in lower Manhattan near the heart of SoHo, I stared out the taxi window, studying every exit, building, face, and element.

Wilson interrupted me with a flurry of texts.

> *Where are you?*
>
> *How close are you to the hotel?*
>
> *There is a change of plans.*
>
> *We are going to meet at DJ's house.*
>
> *Call me when you can.*

Who was DJ, and why did I need to meet with him? Was he important, and if so, why? As I approached the hotel, I removed my BlackBerry from my pocket, read the most recent text message, and audibly gasped. His final text stopped me in my tracks.

> *Oh, by the way, DJ is Derek Jeter. You'll be taking over his shoe when I leave. I'm meeting with him today, and I want to introduce you in person so we have a smooth handoff.*

I stood in front of the hotel in shock, realizing I was about to meet one of the greatest baseball athletes, and I would soon be directly responsible for his ability to compete at the highest level. I would be his dedicated designer. Strangely, this outcome was inevitable. Here I was, a young Black man from the south side of Chicago who desired to become Dr. Lucius Fox in Gotham City, meeting the real-life Bruce Wayne.

This fortunate outcome brought me to tears. After years of patience, a release of fear and rejection streamed down my face; the doorman approached me to ask if I was okay. He seemed noticeably concerned. I had barely left the taxi before I broke down. His concern for me was refreshing and affirming. I shared the news with him, feeling the need to receive love and care from an elder.

He was moved to tears as I spoke about my journey and my trials and tribulations.

He removed his hat, extended his arms, and embraced me with the warmth of a grandfather. Then, in a thick Caribbean accent, he said, "I'm proud of you, son. I am so proud of you. As a Black man and a child of God, you are obviously blessed. Your parents and your ancestors are so proud of you. Hell, I don't even know you, and I'm proud of you."

It was as if I was the physical manifestation of his goals. I was the embodiment of the "American Dream," the thing that brought him from his native home to a foreign land in pursuit of a better life for his progeny.

We shook hands and laughed about our shared experience as I gathered my belongings and emotions while entering the hotel's large iron-and-glass front doors, preparing to abandon my luggage and rush to my pending date with destiny.

After checking in, I hurried to my room to rummage through my bags for the perfect outfit. Earlier that week, I had made plans to meet with my friend Jonathan, a.k.a. Hovain, an ambitious Brooklyn native I met while visiting my sister at Howard University the previous year. He offered to join me as I gathered market insights, connected with the culture, and soaked up the natural energy of a New York summer.

He was fascinated with my career path and desire to transcend our collective circumstances while forging a way forward that allowed others to see themselves in my example. I immediately texted Hovain to coordinate a meeting time and hit the streets.

> *Peace, bro; where are you at today? You still good to link?*

> *What's good? Absolutely. Let's link on Atlantic Ave. When you are ready.*

Our plans were set. I would meet Hovain, buy an outfit, and proceed to Jeter's apartment across town.

When I arrived in Brownsville, Brooklyn, I remembered Hovain's stories of his horrific past. But, until that point, my only frame of reference was M.O.P.'s song "Ante Up," which vividly described the complex intricacies of life in Brooklyn.

Hovain met me at the curb of his apartment building, hopped in the cab, and we were off to explore the city. As he explained the history of his hometown, it dawned on me that I was in a position to share a unique moment with a young Black man who could greatly benefit from an alternative perspective.

We were both in a moment where our ambitions were beyond our opportunities, but Wilson had presented me with a path upward, and I wanted to pay it forward immediately.

I invited Hovain to shadow me for the entirety of my day. I wanted to ensure I had someone who understood my upbringing, my perspective of the world, and, more importantly, my desire not to become a statistic.

I pulled out my phone and texted Wilson.

> *I am with my cousin. Would you mind if he came? He's a native New Yorker, a good dude, and could benefit from seeing someone like you and Jeter. I know I have.*

Without hesitation, he responded.

> *Absolutely. I would love to meet him. Jete said it was okay as well.*

Before I even met DJ, he graciously extended his offer to my friend, enabling us both to see another level of Black excellence that seemed unobtainable to our limited worldview.

I turned to Hovain with a giant grin and said, "Change of plans. Are you a Yankees fan?"

In true New York fashion, he responded, "Son. Are you serious? I'm not from Queens. Of course I f—— with the Yankees."

I burst into laughter because I understood the nuanced significance of his response. It was the equivalent of someone asking a person from the south side of Chicago if they were a White Sox fan. Sports teams serve as a proxy for community pride and social orientation when you travel around the world. Our beloved sports teams represent the highest form of human aspiration.

When they win, we all win.

After laughing nonstop for a few minutes, I shared the news with him. We would be meeting with Derek Jeter, and he was invited to join. A subtle grin emerged on his face, and in a calm Brooklyn demeanor, he responded, "That's what's up."

"Ayo, change of plans," I blurted out, alerting the driver to our new destination. "We need to head to Manhattan for a meeting."

We were on our way. My excitement was building, but I felt prepared for the moment. We traversed the city, weaving in and out of traffic until we arrived at Jeter's building. The sleek, monolithic architectural marvel was neatly situated among a small cluster of buildings that numerous people of great personal wealth occupied. We entered and provided our names and identification to the lobby security guard, who stood idly by, anticipating our arrival.

"Mr. Wilson Smith and Mr. Gentry Humphrey are over there. You two are all clear. Head to the elevator, and it will take you to the seventy-second floor." His tone was confident and respectful.

Is this what it feels like to be wealthy and famous? Do people get paid to speak with a kind and calm tone? I thought.

I walked with the amazement of a young child entering an amusement park for the first time. Every subtle detail, surface, texture, and decorative element radiated a sense of luxury and value.

"Who else lives here?" I asked.

Gentry, the footwear product director for Jordan Brand, swiftly replied as we entered the awaiting destination elevator, "On Jete's floor, it's just him, Bill Gates, and Jay-Z."

"Well d——n!" Hovain replied.

As we ascended to the seventy-second floor, I thought back on what I had experienced a few months earlier and where my career was leading me.

Here we were, standing with two successful Black men who had been given instructions from my hero, Michael Jordan, to ensure I was covered for the meeting.

I was fortunate to experience that level of excellence and camaraderie among my people. MJ believed if we behaved like family, we could become the first billion-dollar athletic brand with a Black man as its core representative. I was living in the vision of the Cleveland summit.

Aligned, connected, strong, and proudly Black, we arrived at the seventy-second floor. Now I would transition to the next journey stage.

The door to Jeter's apartment was a single piece of dark wood. It stood out from the soft, muted color palette that framed the hallway. We approached the door, which opened slowly, revealing a panoramic and surreal view of New York City at dusk.

We entered, and I noticed the precious monuments of his professional career on my left. ESPY awards, Golden Gloves, World Series trophies, rings, and more adorned the shelves and walls of his living quarters. The setting sun gently danced across the surface of each artifact, reflecting and refracting, leading the eye from left to right until they finally settled on an enigmatic figure standing silently with his back facing us.

Dressed in the chic ensemble of black trousers, a black cashmere mock neck, and beautifully crafted Italian loafers, he stood proudly overlooking the city he had sworn to defend against his athletic foes.

Derek Jeter was the actual manifestation of Bruce Wayne. He was an elegant athletic socialite who deeply cared for the well-being of the community he served.

Seconds later, his house manager escorted us to where we would meet. As we approached, DJ turned around and dapped us up like we were teammates. "Welcome to the fam, Jason. Heard great things about you, young buck. Looking forward to working."

He was enthusiastic about meeting the new kid.

"The feeling is mutual, man," I replied. "Really grateful for the opportunity. By the way, this is Jonathan, and I appreciate you allowing him to be here as well."

"Nice to meet you as well, Jonathan. Glad to have you here, man," Jeter said as we sat to begin our meeting.

"Thank you for the invite. It's crazy to be here. I appreciate it, man," Hovain calmly replied.

Throughout the evening, we discussed Jeter's life, his approach to baseball, and my journey from the south side of Chicago to the seventy-second floor. What Wilson provided for me that day was a tangible example of what it meant to be a blessing while you are waiting on your blessings.

Over the last twenty years, I have sought to live a life of honor and gratitude as a form of appreciation for Wilson's and Derek's belief in me.

That day changed our lives forever.

Today, Hovain is one of the most successful entrepreneurs in the music industry. He routinely travels the world, finding unique talent and providing them with opportunities to live their dreams. In addition, he is a husband, father, legendary executive, and community leader who has carried the energy forward from that brisk September afternoon.

Wilson saw and acknowledged the divinity within my being, and in turn, I recognized the same in Hovain.

Two lives were changed that day by one simple act from a humble man who desired to be a blessing in our time of need. Through his example, I found a renewed sense of hope and confidence.

The rise of the Jumpman had begun.

CHAPTER 11

A BILLI

True love accelerates your life.

Sonny and I evolved from friends to parents of two exceptional children. We got married and successfully purchased our first home. We broke generational curses while creating the foundation for a life that would honor our ancestors' sacrifices while inspiring our offspring's future aspirations.

In less than five years since I returned to Beaverton, I had ascended from a designer in Cross Training to a tenured senior designer in Jordan Brand. I was responsible for designing innovative initiatives for athletes such as Derek Jeter, Carmelo Anthony, April Holmes, Andre Ward, and Michael Jordan. As the brand evolved, MJ successfully transitioned from a player to an executive. He wanted to lead us to become the first Black-led sports brand to reach $1 billion in annual sales.

We explored the intersections of culture, technology, and sport by including accurate three-dimensional representations of Jordan footwear in video games such as NBA Live and NBA 2K. In addition, I led creative collaborations with musical artists such as T.I., Lil Wayne, Eminem, and 9th Wonder. The various aspects of my interest converged into one expression of creativity.

I was living my childhood dream alongside my wife and my son. I had defied the odds and proudly crossed over the age of twenty-five.

As I continued to ascend, I set my sights on evolving beyond the limiting title of footwear designer. But unfortunately, I felt trapped in a corporate system that limited the impact of Black creatives. I often felt the weight of an impenetrable glass ceiling that existed to penalize my curiosity and limit the grandeur of my aspirations.

Longing to be viewed as a multi-hyphenate creative capable of adding value in various areas of the company, I traveled the world learning Nike's operating model. From development centers in Taiwan to distribution centers in Belgium, I had an insatiable desire to contribute to the business's strategy, not just the brand's relevance. This interest in business pulled me toward graduate school.

My team and I would often pull all-nighters in pursuit of being remembered by history. With our efforts combined, we strived to become legendary.

For some, this meant burnout and fatigue. For others, this meant evolution and resolve. But no matter how the work impacted us, we were a family, aligned with one vision and purpose.

We had all temporarily set aside our personal goals for the betterment of the collective. I delayed my pursuit of attending graduate school until we reached our financial goals. MJ wanted to make history, and I wanted to bring my family's name into the highest echelon of academia and business. Our shared destiny bound us together.

Managing the workload of a senior designer for two of the world's greatest athletes is an exercise in time management and strategic planning. It requires time, attention to detail, and an extraordinarily uncommon level of persistence.

I was studying for the GMAT, LSAT, and GRE; designing shoes for Chris Paul, Derek Jeter, and Michael Jordan; and awaiting the arrival of my second child.

An advanced degree would be my way of expanding my network beyond the industry that had enamored me since childhood. In addition, I wanted broad exposure to diverse leadership styles, intelligence, and skill.

While running track in high school, Coach Daniels often told me that to run faster, you first have to be willing to run with people faster than you. I craved further expansion of my intellectual rigor and leadership development; I needed to disrupt my place of comfort in pursuit of growth. Five evenings a week, I rushed home to share a meal with my family and assist my wife in creating a harmonious atmosphere before rushing off for three hours of tutor sessions.

During this period, I also traveled back home to Chicago to present my initial concept for the Air Jordan 2009 to MJ himself in the home he occupied while dominating the worlds of basketball and pop culture.

Upon my arrival, I was thrilled. Finally, I had come to what many Chicagoans would regard as hallowed ground. The home's front entrance had an imposing, stainless steel gate emblazoned with the number twenty-three in the exact font used on his official uniform. As we entered the gates, I noticed a manicured putting green directly across from the main house and his garage, which housed various exotic supercars.

The house manager, who had eagerly awaited our arrival, escorted us from our vehicle into his front room. Flanked by Gentry Humphrey and Dale Allen, heads of Sports Marketing for Jordan, I anxiously entered the home of my childhood hero.

I was visiting Mount Olympus, and the feeling was surreal. With each step, I surveyed the home, taking mental images of places immortalized in photos chronicling his heroic achievements: the couch where he sat with his family in the book *Rare Air*, the mythical "Trophy Room," a circular enclave that housed the center court of the original Madhouse on Madison, the Air Jordan 3s from the 1988 dunk contest, numerous Olympic gold medals, O'Brien trophies, MVP awards, Wheaties boxes, and more. Being given a narrated tour of MJ's home by the man himself was overwhelming.

"MJ, may I use your restroom?" I asked, hoping to hide my excitement in the immense gravity of the moment. I needed to call my family to share it with them.

"Yep, it's down the hall on the right. When you are done, we can meet in the conference room to the left," he replied in a comforting voice. He was used to people being nervous around him. He was even more used to me relishing every moment we interacted with one another.

By the grace of God, I was standing next to my hero on common ground.

I entered the bathroom, shut the door, and pretended to use the restroom. Seconds turned to minutes as I described every detail to my mother, who listened intently to every word.

"Mom, he has a Jumpman on his towels. *On his towels!* This is crazy; I cannot believe I made it, Mom. I did it," I whispered with the enthusiasm of a child receiving his entire wish list on Christmas.

As time passed, I heard a knock on the door. "Young buck, tell your mom I said hello and made sure you washed your hands."

The acoustics in the bathroom had betrayed me. Anyone standing a few feet away from the door overheard my entire conversation.

Embarrassed by this revelation, I said goodbye to my mom. Then, I sheepishly exited the bathroom, expecting to be ridiculed for my decision to share the details of my experience with the one person who deserved to hear it the most.

I wanted to give her the gift of hearing her neurodivergent child who sometimes felt "othered" finally stand in his moment. She deserved to listen to the words: "Mom, I did it! I grew up to design shoes for Michael Jordan."

MJ shared a story of a similar moment with his family. He understood the importance and power of including our parents in our accomplishments. To my surprise, he was not mad at all. There he stood, grinning ear to ear, waiting with open arms to dap me up and congratulate me.

"Man, that was awesome. You should feel proud. You should share this with your parents. You did it, kid. You did it." Years of ridicule for holding on to a vision no one else could see was all erased with his straightforward phrase. "You did it, kid. You did it."

Gentry and Dale stood by, laughing and encouraging me to share the inspiration for my concept. They were immersed in my moment as well. They shared a love for MJ and the brand. They knew what this meant to my family and me, and they wanted me to be present for it all. For an hour, we discussed the project's vision. We aspired to create a shoe that leveraged the art of defense as inspiration. Inspired by April Holmes, the inverted carbon fiber plate improved propulsion and forward motion.

MJ was an athletic predator, stronger, faster, and more cunning than his competition. His defense was his greatest attribute and served as a source of inspiration during the design of the Air Jordan. Our short but informative meeting gave me the proper encouragement and understanding for what he needed in a performance product.

When we returned to Beaverton, I worked frantically to establish a proper foundation for an innovative research plan while managing the needs of my growing family, a rapidly developing business, and a rigorous test-prep regimen. Stress and anxiety came in waves.

How was I supposed to maintain the well-being of my family on one income?

How would I live up to my expectations as an employee, man, father, and husband?

I wrestled with feelings of inadequacy often. I felt as if the entire weight of the world was bearing down on my chest. Long nights of study after long days of design caused a rapid deterioration of my energy and resilience.

As the year progressed, Jordan Brand was well toward its economic goals. Nike began to establish its category offense, and critical leaders like Jordan Brand's president, Larry Miller, were starting to depart on new adventures, having climbed the highest mountain in sports and apparel with limited resources.

I had a different outcome.

One afternoon, while folding clothes in the hallway of our home, I felt a wave of emotion and collapsed to the floor. Barely able to stand, I crawled to the bedroom door, pulled myself up, and called out for Sonny.

"Babe! Babe, I don't feel good. I feel light-headed. I can't see," I murmured as I gathered my bearings. "I need to go to the emergency room."

The intensity of my personal and professional commitments temporarily led me to lose vision in my left eye. Finally, carrying so much physical, mental, and emotional stress led to an implosion.

Months earlier, my aunt had an aneurysm. I was afraid her condition could be a function of genetics and not stress. I needed to know if I would be okay. I needed to make it.

Upon our arrival to the hospital, I was rushed into a small, dimly lit room, given a set of clothes, and informed that a doctor would see me immediately. But first, they needed to perform a spinal tap to extract meningeal fluid to determine if I had an aneurysm.

My wife, three-year-old son, and eight-month-old daughter helplessly watched me taken away in a wheelchair. I held my composure as I left the room. "I love you, babe. I'm fine. I'm fine, kids. I'll be right back." It took every fiber of my being not to break down. I was afraid my ambition had caused irreparable damage to my body. Despite how much we strive, our body keeps the score of the actual cost of success.

I sat alone, waiting as the nurse prepared the needles.

Drenched in sweat, thoughts of leaving my family behind filled my mind with worry. I practiced breathing exercises, attempting to calm myself to bring me back to peace.

One, two, three, four . . . I counted in my mind as I inhaled deeply, hoping to soothe my emotional pain.

"Hey, keep breathing. It's going to be fine," the doctor said as he entered the room. "I've done thousands of these; you'll be fine. Just relax. It will hurt, but I'm here to walk you through it."

His words were not comforting at all.

He prepared the area surrounding my spine by covering it with iodine. I took a deep breath and closed my eyes.

"Alright, here we go," the doctor said. He attempted to insert the needle into my spine. "Ugh, that's weird. Okay, hold on."

"What do you mean *weird*? What's wrong?" I asked with concern. The last thing you want to hear when someone places a needle in your spine is the phrase "that's weird."

The needles bent each time he attempted to penetrate my spinal column. He was unsure how this could happen.

Was it my spinal density? Were the needles defective?

He was baffled.

"I don't want to keep poking around and cause nerve damage. This is strange. I'm so sorry. We can find out what's going on more comfortably."

He left the room and requested a CT scan to prevent any damage from a failed spinal extraction. I sat up, strolled over to the hospital bed, and fell silent. I was shocked and terrified.

"Let's get you prepped for your scan." The nurse pushed me toward the door.

"What's next?" I asked.

"Well, it's pretty simple; we inject you with iodine, and the CT scan's contrast image lets us know if something is going."

When we arrived at the CT scan room, the radiologist placed a lead vest over my chest, instructing me to lie on my back with my eyes closed.

The buzzing sound of the machine warming up served as white noise. As I entered the machine, a sense of calmness overtook me. In some strange way, this afforded me a moment to rest and reflect. I had been running on fumes for months, and this was the first time I found myself in a quiet place with no distractions.

"Okay. All done. We are going to take you back to your family now." The scan was complete, and the nurse would now return me to the care of my family, who were eagerly waiting to find out if I was okay.

"Thank God, babe. We missed you. Are you okay?" Sonny was relieved I was back in the room, but I could sense she was highly concerned about the outcome of the scan. As the nurse prepped my bed, she asked, "Can you tell us anything? Is he okay?"

"It should only be a few minutes. The doctor usually has results within thirty minutes or less. Just hold tight. From what we can tell so far, he is okay."

After almost a half hour, the doctor returned to my bedside.

"The scan was a success. We found no signs of anything serious happening to your husband. From talking with him, we think it's related to his work. So that's a good thing." His words provided a sense of relief for Sonny and me.

They determined my loss of vision was due to intense stress. I was working myself to death, literally. When the doctor noticed the concern on my son's face, he told my family he had good and bad news. "The good news is your dad is made out of adamantium." That was the fictional alloy from Marvel's *X-Men* comic book series. "The bad news is he needs to slow down. It's not good for his health to keep working like this." He used humor to address the abnormal outcome of the failed spinal extraction and the destructive nature of my work habits. His tone changed as he turned to me. "What are you doing to yourself, young man? Is your job worth your life? Look over there; that is what matters most. You do not owe Nike, grad school, or anyone else your life." His words revealed the flaw in my logic. I was working to prove people wrong rather than to prove God right. I had lost sight of my *why*.

When we returned home, I took the next week to rest and recalibrate before deciding which path to take. Ultimately, I decided to pursue my master's in business. I wanted to understand how to build business models, not just 3D models.

I would attend business school to expand my reach and diversify my opportunities. I ran my race with Jordan Brand and Nike. I would shift my focus toward the advancement of my family and my community.

That year, 2008, was a year of revelation and change for me. However, the remaining months required extreme focus and discipline. Rumors of mass layoffs across corporate America due to a collapsing economy had dominated the headlines. I felt scared and exhausted. I needed to be fully rested and ready to take my GMAT.

Summer was ending, and the test day had finally arrived. It was August; I was well ahead of the October application deadlines. After that, I had to take the test, submit the scores to my desired schools, complete my application, and wait for a response in early 2009.

With mounting financial uncertainty and the responsibilities of providing for a young family, I often found myself overcome with worry despite my previous encounter with fatigue and stress.

The vision of my desired life was getting harder to believe. I could only see to the corner of my desires, but God saw around the corner. He knew I would need extreme faith to endure.

What happened next would forever change my life and the depths of my faith.

CHAPTER 12

DELAYED DOES NOT MEAN DENIED

The pursuit of a vision often leads you down uncomfortable paths.

Each twist and turn tests your patience, stretches your faith, and challenges your endurance. It helps to dig deep to find consistency in your approach and drive. Beyond the accolades resides your *why*. For me, it was and still is my love for my family. I wanted to set an example that would energize my children to live authentically and intentionally.

The application process for grad school was a blur. I had successfully taken the GMAT and narrowed down my top choices to Harvard Business School and Chicago Booth School of Business while continuing to compile all of the required documents requested of prospective students. However, despite my progress, my spirit felt unsettled.

We were a family of four, a single-income household, and had absolutely no community to embrace us if we moved east. Chicago was the most logical option, but I was not ready to move back home. Instead, I wanted to explore the world, gather more insights, and return when I had the financial means and the position to make systemic change.

While pondering my path forward, I informed D'Wayne Edwards, now a well-respected director within Nike, of my plans. He warned me that sharing my desire to leave for grad school before Nike officially announced a layoff could put me at risk for termination.

Overwhelmed with despair and concern, I returned home that evening and sat mostly silent as I watched my son play without hesitation. His freedom came at the cost of my expended energy. He was the best part of me, and I wanted to show and not just tell him about the power of sacrificial love.

The night progressed, and my wife retreated to our room to rest. She was feeling fatigued after tending to the needs of our daughter. I put my son to bed and returned to my room where I lay down, staring at the ceiling, uncertain of my fate.

Should I quit? Is it foolish to expose my family to this financial risk? Boston is not the best place for us, but if I get into Harvard, I can change my trajectory.

Those questions swirled in my mind. I felt like a failure for even considering giving up. The role of a Black father was to sacrifice his time, well-being, and resources for the betterment of his family. In some cases, this self-sacrificial role would lead a Black father to offer his life for his loved ones.

With tears streaming down my face, I dozed off, only partially awakened by a bright, warm, and affectionate light. I could not tell if I was dreaming or if this experience was a lucid reality intended to reveal the presence of God's grace surrounding me.

As I arose, I heard what sounded like every voice in the history of the world singing in a beautiful, concise tone, followed by a familiar voice. "Trust me. Will you trust me?"

Startled and partially stuck between my imagination and reality, I returned to sleep, dismissing this experience as a mere dream. I responded to the call to trust, but I did not fully believe this was a divine message.

It could only be a dream.

Upon waking, I had a nagging feeling I should check my email. Each morning, I would routinely pray and meditate before letting the world pull me in. However, the urge to browse my inbox was growing by the second. So I unlocked my BlackBerry and scrolled from the top of my inbox until I saw an email from my mentor, Gina Warren, the chief diversity officer of Nike.

> *I know this sounds strange, but I could not stop thinking about you last night. Can you talk today? Have you ever considered going to grad school? Call me when you get this message.*

I was astonished. I had decided the night before to abandon my pursuit of my master's to maintain my employment with Nike. I needed a way to provide for my family while attending school full-time, and this was highly unlikely. How did she know I was pursuing this path? I had only told D'Wayne, and he assured me our conversation would remain between us as friends. He was a man of his word, so this had to be divine intervention. I was at a loss for words. I called her immediately.

"Hey, what's up, Gina? What's going on?" I asked with enthusiasm.

Gina was often the source of good news. A brilliant Black woman, she dedicated her life and career to advancing pathways for underrepresented groups in corporate America. She was known as "Auntie Gina" because of her friendly disposition and affirming spirit.

"Jason, I have to tell you, I had the strangest urge to call you last night and ask you a question, but first, I want to hear how you are doing. How's your family?" She customarily asked to get a sense of your well-being before she launched into prophesying over your career.

"I'm well. We are all good. Our kids are healthy; I'm just working hard. Sonny is feeling okay, and we are blessed. What's up your way? What did you want to talk about?" I replied anxiously, waiting to hear the wisdom in her words.

"Well, have you ever thought about going to grad school? Nike has a program at Stanford, and if you get accepted, they pay for your salary and benefits while you study. This would be great for you, but you need a sponsor."

I gasped, realizing maybe my dream the previous night was more of a revelation from God intended to comfort me as I deepened my trust in his plan for my life.

"Gina, what's crazy is I just chose to end my pursuit of getting into Harvard last night. I had a great informal interview, and the alum I spoke with even mentioned I might have a better time at Stanford as a creative—or a 'Mac person,' as he called it—and maybe I should apply there instead. This is a blessing. Yes, I would love to do it."

We sat in silence, amazed by the power of our alignment. At the same time the previous night, we were both given unusual instructions. Our fear led us to question the calling; our faith compelled us to continue our inquiry.

The possibility of attending Stanford while maintaining provision for my family was compelling. Weeks went by as I urgently reviewed the application requirements and prepared my recommendation letters, test scores, and essays for submission. It was late September 2008, and I only had a few more weeks before my window of opportunity would close. I rushed to apply before the deadline, fully committed to competing with the world for a coveted spot at the Stanford Graduate School of Business. It was now time to wait again.

In my haste, I failed to appreciate the nuanced nature of how someone should go about applying for sponsored employee opportunities. Instead, I viewed everything as a meritocracy.

I was surprised to find out an executive on the CEO's team was supposed to nominate me. Applying without notifying the proper executives was not an intentional act of defiance. I believed in my abilities and intelligence. I wanted to get into Stanford on merit alone.

Weeks turned to months, and I had yet to hear back from Stanford. During the waiting period, my family and I visited the campus for an in-person informational interview. Palo Alto was the home of my wife's family. Her mother was the child of Italian immigrants who moved west for a better life. In a way, acceptance to Stanford would serve as a return home for her.

Everything was in divine order.

Meanwhile, the climate at Nike had an unsettling feeling of pending professional upheaval. In February 2009, rumors surfaced that Nike was planning to announce a round of layoffs intended to sharpen our focus and reduce the company's operational expenses. In addition, we were entering into an economic collapse due to the stock market crash the previous year.

The crisis-caused financial turmoil impacted many sectors, leading to massive job losses and mortgage defaults. As investment firms collapsed and automakers stood on the verge of bankruptcy, the federal government stepped in and bailed out company after company (Lusk 2019).

Nike was not immune to the market crash. Sales dropped, budgets were cut, and executive leadership scrutinized every job in hopes of preserving enough cash to weather the storm.

I powered forward despite the uncertainty. I had yet to get word from Stanford, and I was growing more impatient by the day. I needed an answer. I was curious to know if I would head to Palo Alto, lose my job, or be asked to stay instead of pursuing my graduate degree if I had been accepted to Stanford.

Employees nervously entered work each day. Every email, call, and interaction triggered a sense of anxiety.

We all nervously waited for our verdicts.

My life was held in suspense, personally and professionally.

Once again, I was in the waiting place.

Months later, on May 15, 2009, the waiting finally ended. Nike announced that 1,750 jobs, including 500 at the world headquarters in Oregon, would be cut (Rogoway 2009). Lay-offs were beginning, my workload was increasing, and I was afraid I would be terminated because of my desire to attend grad school.

Every phone call brought great concern. Employees were asked to meetings via email with no subject, only to return to their desks in shambles. Security would accompany them while they placed their belongings into a box. The Nike dream was fading away to reveal the Nike business.

I kept my head down, stayed focused, and remained calm. I remembered the gentle whisper of God's voice in my vision. I continued to trust him, even in times of doubt. As colleagues who decided to accept their severance filled my inbox with notes of anger, sadness, and well wishes, I was shocked to receive a meeting request from David Ayer, Nike's chief human resource officer.

Stanford had informed him of my application during a visit to their campus to discuss the details of their executive sponsorship program. He was stunned that I, as a designer, had successfully gained admittance to the world's most prestigious business school without leaning into Nike's politics. I had earned my way, and he was furious the committee did not select me.

God elected me.

The meeting would take place the following morning. When I arrived at David's office, I scanned the room, searching for artifacts that gave me insight into how he saw the world. Artifacts of his love for hockey, small collectibles from successful Nike collaborations, and neatly curated culture books were on full display.

He obviously wanted to be creative and approachable. His office was a mixture of personal pride for his family and home country of Canada interwoven with his educational accreditation and framed news articles that highlighted his various professional accolades.

As I entered the room, he said, "So, you're a pretty hot topic these days. Heard a lot about you from Stanford. They are excited to have a designer join the program. Why should we use a hammer when we can use a screwdriver? Don't you think it's easier and cheaper if we send you to a new category to learn how to be a leader? What if we sent you to running? That's the heart of Nike. Why Stanford?"

As I listened to his barrage of questions, I felt an overwhelming sense of peace.

Briefly pausing to gather my thoughts, I replied in a firm and polite tone, "Well, considering Nike is a global company, I believe it is important for leaders to learn and leverage insights from other organizations, not just product lines. I want to gain knowledge to implement upon my return. I want to be a globally minded leader who can bring relevancy to our work, not just what we work on." My answer was quick, clear, and specific.

After my accurate, honest response, he tilted his head curiously to the right, disarmed. "Well, I see why everyone believes in you. That's the perfect answer. I guess you're going to Stanford. Congratulations. I'll pass along my approval today. Make us proud, young man."

That was it. I was heading to Stanford. I had no clue David was the deciding vote. Had I not felt confident enough to defend my aspirations, I would have unintentionally blocked my blessings.

"Oh, by the way, we were informed of your acceptance before we made you aware. I know it must have sucked to hear nothing after the deadline. I'm sure you can understand the sensitive position I was in. I appreciate how you handled this meeting."

This revelation showed his questions were a litmus test to see if my aspirations were real. He needed to feel like he had decided to approve my sponsorship.

I was unaware of the back-channel politics accompanying these executive development opportunities. I lived in the meritocratic bubble of design, where your impact on the bottom line quantifies your worth. I did not have to navigate a world where a person's network served as a proxy for their organizational worth. I was used to doing the work to advance.

I sprinted across campus toward my desk, but before I could sit down to call my wife, D'Wayne intercepted me outside his office. "Do you have a minute?" he asked.

"Yep, what's up?" I replied.

"So we are sending you to Stanford, but I couldn't tell you. I found out last week. Apparently, Nike found out in February. However, you have to make a choice. You can't go this year. We need you to defer for a year. You have two signature shoes, and we are down a designer with layoffs."

I immediately felt an overwhelming sense of calm. I knew what God had for me would not be denied. I had reached a place of profound inner peace that allowed me to accept that my reality resulted from my faith and ability to manifest beyond limitations. I asked for twenty-four hours to pray and respond. I needed time to process the impact of my decision on my family and career.

Ultimately, my wife and I decided to pursue a path that forced us to rely solely on God. The following day, I informed D'Wayne I had decided to stay, despite not having a firm offer. I had the vision God gave me, and I was determined to attend Stanford with or without Nike's support.

Moreover, I had a promise from MJ himself. He was committed to ensuring I would attend Stanford if I stayed. He had honored his word numerous times in the past. A vow of support from someone you admire gives you a sense of relief. When MJ said, "I got you," he meant it.

The following twelve months would be one of my best years. Every shoe I designed broke records and unlocked significant value for the brand. I was on fire. I created new concepts with the veracity of a man destined to leave a legacy. I was determined to not only prove I was qualified and capable of being a leader, but I was also determined to leave Jordan Brand on a high note.

My efforts resulted in design's version of a game-winning jump shot.

Life was becoming more precious by the minute. Finally, we had a new direction; our family began to plan for our move to Palo Alto.

When the time came for me to collect on MJ's promise, Jordan Brand provided overwhelming support. Phil Knight and MJ had aligned to share the cost of my advanced degree personally. I would receive a salary, benefits, and a chance to continue working on my final shoe with Chris Paul.

Miracles do not come from brute force. Instead, miracles are born amid great patience and long-suffering.

As a young professional, I believed in the power of delayed gratification. What the world deemed impossible, God deemed possible.

I defied the odds. I broke the mold. I changed the trajectory of my life.

I was becoming the first me rather than the next anyone else.

CHAPTER 13

GASSED UP

You either win or you learn.

Stanford University is known as "the Farm." Its storied history and sprawling campus were intimidating at first glance.

It is a place of innovation and privilege. It feels a world apart from the blocks I roamed as a teenager on the south side of Chicago. My tireless effort to advance had brought my family and me to the south bay of San Francisco.

The transition to northern California required a perspective, pace, and comfort shift. We moved from our newly built first home into modest graduate housing Stanford had not renovated since the mid-1980s. Escondido Village would be the place of our new adventure. As we settled into our humble abode, we often gathered informally with our new peers to enhance a sense of community.

Each interaction with my classmates reinforced my imposter syndrome. Their résumés and accolades read like excerpts from *Forbes*—successful entrepreneurs, wealthy management consultants, tech executives, high-ranking government officials, and me, a footwear designer from Jordan. I was still determining what I had to offer as an industrial designer in an environment fueled by data and technical analysis.

In the hallowed halls of Silicon Valley, scientific inquiry drove invention, not youthful creative expression. So, like many students at prestigious universities, I believed my admission to Stanford might have been a mistake.

I struggled with imposter syndrome.

People who suffer from this self-deprecating mindset are defined as those "who believe that they are undeserving of their achievements and the high esteem in which they are, in fact, generally held. They feel that they aren't as competent or intelligent as others might think—and that soon enough, people will discover the truth about them. Those with imposter syndrome are often well accomplished; they may hold high office or have numerous academic degrees" (Psychology Today Staff 2022).

I had never been around a concentrated group of highly accomplished professionals who often enjoyed generational wealth privileges.

"What do you do?"

"Where did you go to undergrad?"

"Where did you grow up?"

Every question felt like an assessment of the legitimacy of my admittance and worth.

At Stanford, failure was a rite of passage, and intelligence and critical discourse were the norms. Being a nerd was considered desirable.

Trials were growing me.

Undertaking advanced courses in econometrics, finance, and negotiations overwhelmed me with new frameworks and a profound understanding of managerial science.

My brain swelled as I searched for the intersection of the disparate concepts I was learning. I found inspiration in everything.

The thought that someone with my skill set had no place in entrepreneurship eroded as I read through countless case studies proving the market value of a design-led organization.

Creativity was indeed present in business operations.

I was no longer bound to a function or a service; I could lead organizations and build companies that leveraged design as a defensible differentiator in the market. My fondest childhood memories revolved around my time with my father when he was a student at Chicago State. Mere exposure to the collegiate environment made it possible for me to see myself as capable. I wanted to replicate this with my children to ensure they knew their privilege's actual cost.

I commonly attended class with my son sitting patiently on my lap, sketching, listening, and observing each interaction. Simply in the exposure to a radically advanced environment, his mind expanded.

In our household, we did not frame any outcome as impossible. On the contrary, the intrinsic evidence of our ancestral perseverance allowed us to see things in varying degrees of difficulty.

In our mind, nothing was impossible for God.

Weekend visits to museums were testing grounds for my children's ability to decipher the meaning of an image through discernment and discourse. At ages two and six, they learned how to assess and critique art. We purposefully prepared their minds to question the world around them.

With my children, I decided to replace the ritual of popcorn and Adam West's *Batman* with smoothies and readings from *The Columbian Orator*, a collection of timeless essays, orations, and poetry used to instruct students in the art of public speaking during the nineteenth century.

This proud collection of the world's greatest orations was also the book Frederick Douglass used to teach himself how to read. In between study groups, I sat with my son, reading each speech, pausing to ask, "Do you know what that word means?" to instill in him a sense of curiosity and permission.

"No," he responded as he clung to my arm, wrestling with his desire to move.

"Okay, well, let's underline it, write it down, look up the definition, and then use it in a sentence." Despite his age, I knew learning was a function of exposure, not aptitude. The more I learned in grad school, the sooner I positioned the content in a context a child would easily understand. We were learning and growing as a unit. I was breaking the cycle and creating a new tradition built on education and grand aspirations.

Unlike the two-year MBA, the Sloan Fellowship was a fast-paced, accelerated program for seasoned executives returning to school after years of operational experience.

People under thirty were not commonly accepted due to their limited managerial experience. However, my time at Nike prepared me for this program. I had the experience to know the trials and tribulations of an organizational leader while maintaining the youthful optimism of a twenty-nine-year-old creative.

As the year progressed, I took on leadership roles with the Black Business Student Association. I led discussions with dignitaries and government officials, established and managed the first TEDx Stanford event, and was invited to give a surprise speech at Phil Knight's induction into the coaches 'hall of fame.

I had come alive intellectually, professionally, and personally.

I was taking on each challenge with faith and certainty.

Being exposed to the Silicon Valley ecosystem changed my interest in working for a large corporation. Everywhere I went, the energy of funding and bringing to life new ideas surrounded me.

This newfound energy led me to enroll in courses like the famed S356: Evaluating Entrepreneurial Opportunities, which broadened my understanding of what was possible for a group of dedicated professionals aligned against a common goal.

Several of my classmates were also deeply passionate about the evolution of sports. So we decided to apply as a team to S356 to explore ideas that could lead to a formal company. Alongside a group of technologists, business operators, and video game designers, we created a conceptual ecosystem of products focused on muscle myography, indoor tracking, real-time coaching, and player workload management.

Our innovation, Kill the Clipboard, a.k.a. KTC, was a novel way to detect and predict the fatigue and possible failure of an athlete while delivering visual feedback in the form of a player-specific, coach-monitored energy meter.

Simply put, we created a real-life video game energy meter for coaches to use conspicuously on the sideline through the newly launched iPad.

Word of our invention had gotten back to Nike, and at the request of Mark Parker, Nike's CEO, two key executives flew to Stanford to speak with me about their plan for a new business unit, Digital Sport. They were in the early days of creating a new category of digital products, services, and experiences and were searching for fresh and innovative approaches to product creation.

My skill set and knowledge positioned me as an ideal candidate for a leading role on the team. Despite my desire to continue with our KTC concept, I ultimately returned to Nike after graduation as the director of innovation for Digital Sport.

My love for technology, design, and human potential intersected at the right moment in my career.

Surprisingly, returning to Nike after this transformational experience was tricky. Digital Sport was a start-up inside an established organization with a forty-year-old business model that had proven lucrative and successful. The mixture of Silicon Valley-trained engineers and Nike-trained brand builders naturally caused creative friction.

It was 2012, and we were working on the future of sport while being held to the product standards firmly established by Nike's success in the 1990s.

While others worked on the latest footwear, my team focused on developing advanced concepts with augmented reality that leveraged GPS data and virtual goods. Additionally, we explored use cases for mobile computer vision powered by machine learning and artificial intelligence that would identify, detect, and assess the wear of shoes. Our goal was to predict when an athlete should buy a replacement pair and automate the process of reducing waste.

Rumors of a new dawn spread around Nike's corporate campus. Born from a group of unlikely innovators tucked away, once again, on the fourth floor of the Jerry Rice building.

Veterans of Nike scoffed at the idea of digitally enhanced goods. For them, Nike was a pinnacle footwear and apparel company—nothing more, nothing less.

The idea of creating a new metric to measure athletic output was a feat no one had ever attempted at this scale. We were replacing calories with fuel points to usher in the era of the "quantified self." This renaissance of personal assessment for well-being had made the rounds in Silicon Valley for several years under the term "biohacking." However, it had now found its way to the home of sports innovation in Beaverton, Oregon.

We were creating solutions to future problems, and I felt right at home despite the chaotic pace.

As a function of my role, I frequently visited Silicon Valley to meet with founders, investors, and tech luminaries. I was determined to endure the complex and highly political environment surrounding Digital Sport. The work, partnerships, and advanced research allowed me to remain closely connected to the world surrounding Stanford.

Despite my outward success, connection to Stanford, and high-profile workload, I still did not feel at peace within my soul. I held the secret of what I experienced deep inside at the age of fourteen. Survivor's remorse intensified with each step I took up the corporate ladder.

I felt guilty for my success and needed to break free from the unfair assumption that I was undeserving because I had survived the traumatic experiences of my childhood. I wanted to thrive, but first, I had to heal.

Through my involvement as a student leader at the inaugural TEDx Stanford, a chance to speak at the conference presented itself the following year.

I knew if I wanted to conquer my guilt and shame, I would first need to confront it. The catalyst for my journey needed to be shared. I was no longer ashamed of my origins.

What could have destroyed me was molding me into an empathetic leader. I accepted the offer and prepared my short talk, which was intended to document the depth of my journey and destigmatize the life of inner-city youth.

On the day of the conference, I nervously paced the back halls of the auditorium. I wondered what would happen when the world found out about my trauma. How would I be judged?

When my time came to present, I took a deep breath, walked boldly onto the red dot positioned center stage, and began to speak. With each word, I could see a range of emotions dance across the audience's faces. They clung to every word for three minutes. They were finding joy and inspiration in my narrative.

"We all have God-given abilities. So I'm here today to talk about how I used my strengths, gifts, and talents to become the first *me* rather than the next anyone else—" I centered my breath and prepared to share my most vulnerable truth.

"*Bang!*" The sound of a gunshot played over the speaker as the correlating word transitioned onto the screen. A woman in the audience, startled by the unexpected sound, muffled her scream.

I paused, giving myself a moment to control my emotions. Then, for the first time publicly, I shared the story of witnessing my friend get shot.

I shared with them the pain I experienced during those fateful one hundred and eighty seconds. No one outside my immediate family knew the pain I had carried with me all those years.

"It was 1994. South side of Chicago. An event that lasted one hundred and eighty seconds would be the catalyst that made me the person I am today." I nervously fumbled over my words as I delivered the details of the most traumatic experience of my life. I wanted to be free of the internal guilt and shame I carried.

Sharing the story was a form of therapy. Speaking about what I hid from the world allowed me to confront the shadows that lingered in my past.

I was finally breaking free.

Upon the conclusion, the crowd erupted into applause, and my love for public speaking was officially born. The response I feared the most did not occur. My reality was more welcoming than my imagination. I was accepted, heralded, and rewarded for my honesty and authenticity.

I was no longer the misfortunate survivor. There I stood, victorious, Black, and entirely free.

Armed with my fresh confidence, I returned to Nike, ready to take on anything that would come my way.

Little did I know, while I was discovering the depths of my potential, MJ was expanding his interest and aspirations for the brand.

It had only been a year since I had returned to Nike from Stanford when my boss, Stefan Olander, told me MJ had made a play to bring me back to Jordan Brand.

He had requested I return to the brand to lead Design and Innovation. And in an instant, my time in Digital Sport was closing.

I was returning to the Jordan Brand to change the game.

CHAPTER 14

BACK LIKE JORDAN

We rise as one.

Michael Jeffrey Jordan is one of the greatest athletes of all time. However, he was much more than an athlete. Michael is a business strategist who leveraged the sports industry to build an ecosystem of expression that monetized his interest.

He is the original influencer. His style, demeanor, and penchant for design and innovation inspired me my entire life. He carried the blessing and burden of being "our" hero. He represented the hopes and dreams of every young boy and girl in Chicago during a time when examples of excellence were limited.

Michael transcended race, wealth, and regionalism. And as such, Chicago excitedly and reluctantly sent our champion to battle because we knew he would no longer be ours. We knew his brilliance was too great to be hidden from the world. We were all witnesses to Michael's transcendence from a man to a phenomenon to a brand and product adorned with his likeness, the Air Jordan.

Like all great heroes throughout history, Michael faced adversity, self-doubt, and tremendous personal and professional failure. However, despite the complexity of celebrity and the high expectations of a demanding career, Michael rose above his opposition, constantly and fearlessly advancing into the unknown.

He studied the evolution of sports and was curious about the work my team was exploring in Digital Sport. He knew a time would come when Jordan Brand would again have to "zig" while the industry "zagged," as he would often say.

His excitement about the merger of technology and athleticism was rooted in a belief that we could unequivocally prove he was the greatest basketball player of all time through data and analysis.

I was honored and ecstatic to receive an offer to return to Jordan Brand from John Hoke, the Chief Design Officer for Nike. John informed me I was the first director to have an advanced business degree, and I was the youngest designer ever to hold what was regarded at the time to be the most coveted position in all of footwear, head of Design for Jordan. But, unfortunately, the celebration of my return home was short-lived. Colleagues complained about my rapid ascension, and others refused to support my advancement due to the political climate of Nike Design.

The leadership team repositioned my role to Global Design Director to complement the incoming VP/Creative Director. I would have full rein over innovation and footwear design and serve as the interim General Manager for Jordan Basketball, but I would no longer be the creative lead for the entire category.

I had been given the workload without the title. Nevertheless, I gladly accepted the challenge. The Jordan leadership team fully supported me, and I knew, as with everything at Nike, this too was a test.

My journey was a repetitive cycle of "show and prove." The higher I climbed, the more I needed to display the variety of skills I had acquired along the way.

Never ceasing to serve my category and my community, I immediately got to work. I was nominated and elected as co-chair of BEN (Black Employee Network), where I led the redesign and refresh of our brand strategy, which subsequently gave birth to the Sneaker Ball. The premier annual event, held at the end of Black History Month, celebrated the accomplishments of Black employees across the globe. In addition, I continued to contribute to the Doernbecher "Freestyle" project, a relationship I had spearheaded alongside legendary Jordan designer Mark Smith and Doernbecher Children's Hospital in Portland.

Things were taking shape, and as the Global Design Director for Jordan Brand, I displayed my academic and artistic abilities.

The goal of 2013 was to reset the brand. As a result, everything was challenged and redefined as we approached our thirtieth anniversary in 2015.

I leveraged my knowledge of innovation and culture to create a data analysis project intended to dissect the evolving nature of the game.

We hypothesized that if MJ had remained in a constant peak physical state without aging, he would have evolved to dominate his competition in any era of basketball.

The project, entitled "Predator," discovered through topological data analysis that the game itself had evolved into thirteen distinct styles of play, which rendered the previous construct of five athletic positions obsolete.

We had entered an era where seven-footers moved like motorcycles among cars on the court. How we designed, innovated, and positioned our products was being reimagined for the first time since the brand's inception while we extended our reach into culture through partnerships that existed beyond sport.

My network of multi-hyphenate creatives came into play as I used my power and privilege to help establish their brands. Woodie White and Don C are Chicago legends, both known for their contributions to culture and sport.

I met Woodie while spending countless hours in a small Santa Ana office and distribution center that served as the first home of the iconic streetwear brand LRG. Woodie and I became fast friends after discovering our common Chicago roots. Years later, I would again connect with Woodie to establish a deeper relationship with him and Don C. Don had risen through the ranks of culture as one of Kanye's most tenured friends, business affiliates, and collaborators.

His burgeoning brand, Just Don, had a cult following among tastemakers. The hats worn in Chicago's inner city by iconic and infamous urban entrepreneurs inspired creations for celebrities such as Jay-Z. I wanted to leverage my positions in Jordan and BEN to provide a platform for the world to see his gift.

Don C was in love with the brand, and his authentic connection to sports positioned him as one of the first to lead the culture toward retro shoes and throwback sports jerseys. So, we connected and decided the perfect moment to announce our partnership with the world would be during Black History Month in 2013.

The first-of-its-kind collaboration strived to bring awareness to Jordan's philanthropic educational efforts through a vertically integrated partnership with eBay. In addition, Don C would design a version of the Air Jordan 1, limited to thirty-seven pairs, in honor of BHM's thirty-seventh anniversary and a collaborative "Just Jordan" cap with all proceeds going toward Jordan Brand Wings scholarship program.

While working on our project, Don reached out to see if he could provide my phone number to Kanye. The rapper was in the early stages of renegotiating his deal with Nike, and Don had shared the details of our relationship. Don texted me in an attempt to prepare me for an impromptu call.

> *Aye, bro, Ye is going to call you in the next five minutes. He heard you were helping me make moves with Jordan, and he wanted to talk.*

My advocation for Don C's dream to work with Jordan compelled Kanye to make contact in hopes of establishing a formal relationship with Jordan.

Over the next few months, I would oscillate between leading innovation for the Air Jordan 30 project and creating strategies for Jordan's regional offense in New York and Los Angeles while flying back and forth to speak with Kanye at his home in Southern California.

Don C's presence and the essence of Chicago had brought new life to the brand at a time when people felt it had run its course.

The Just Don-Jordan collaboration sold out on launch day in less than a minute. Our project subsequently set the foundation for Jordan to create an independent function dedicated to energy and influencer product partnerships.

Simultaneously, negotiations were intensifying between Kanye and Nike. However, despite the collaboration's outsized success, he felt Nike had purposefully delayed their response to his request for greater resources and support.

During my monthly strategic planning sessions with Nike and Jordan Brand leadership, I shared his frustrations in hopes of finding a mutually beneficial outcome.

"How do you know Kanye?"

"Why is he calling you?"

As expected, a barrage of questions awaited me in every meeting whenever I brought his name up for discussion.

"I am trying to help him live his childhood dream. I met him back in the day through a mutual friend from Chicago, Coodie, and again through Jonas at LRG. It's the perfect story for the brand and the culture. Don C reconnected us. We can't let him leave and go to Adi. It makes zero sense," I often replied, hoping to convince Nike's executive leadership to see the vision of a unified Chicago offense.

My vision was simple. Yeezy Brand would be positioned as a subsidiary of Jordan, and I would oversee the relationship as a colleague and fellow Chicago native.

As the adage goes, "no good deed goes unpunished." My desire to mend the broken relationship between Michael and Kanye spiraled into a battle of control between Nike's entertainment marketing division and Jordan's leadership team, who had been discreetly involved in the discussions from the beginning.

Nike appreciated I was a pseudo-mediator during negotiations; however, territorialism often rebuffs the idea of collective progress in corporate America. Being part of a team with a shared vision is subject to pursuits of individual accolades and safeguarding relationships, and that serves as a barrier to entry for anyone who attempts to add value to convoluted conversations.

After a round of heated conversations with senior executives battling to retain Kanye's allegiance to Nike rather than Jordan, I recused myself from the negotiation. Nevertheless, I successfully provided an opportunity for Don C, and I brokered a discussion for Kanye that could lead to him finally being a part of the brand he had loved since childhood.

Moving on, I focused on my direct reports, their continued personal and professional success, and my continued development as a leader, father, husband, and citizen of the world.

A few weeks went by, and I completely shifted my attention back to the well-being of my team and their exceptionally demanding workload. I fought tirelessly to protect each member of the team and their ability to create using their medium of choice. As a result, everyone in the company was clamoring to visit our space to see the advanced design language that was shifting Jordan into the modern era of sport.

One evening, after a long day of meetings and market travel, I returned home to find my son standing shirtless in the bathroom, staring at himself with a look of defeat. Shockingly, he had gained weight rapidly, and despite our best efforts to live an exceptionally healthy lifestyle, his condition perplexed us. As I embraced him and affirmed his worth, I knew my time at Nike had finally ended. Determining his condition's root cause would require my full attention.

I spent over thirteen years of my life leveraging my talents to help enhance and prolong the careers of the world's greatest athletes. Now my focus would shift to my child. He deserved my best, and no job would come between my responsibilities as a father and a husband, even if that job was the thing I had pursued since I was a child myself.

Sacrifice is the love language of an involved parent, and I was willing to leave it all behind for him. In that instant, I grabbed my phone, texted my friend group, and asked for prayers for clarity as my wife and I planned for my resignation. The memory of watching my father go to work despite his desire to be by my side as I lay in the hospital compelled me to leave.

Over the next few weeks, I shared my decision with critical leaders throughout Nike and Jordan. I wanted them to hear firsthand why I resigned and how I planned to use my time away from Nike. I explained to them I wanted to be with my family, research what my son was experiencing, and ultimately dedicate every waking hour to finding a solution.

My involvement in Kanye's negotiation caused a stir within Nike, so I was conscientious not to publicly share I was resigning before I had the adequate support of key leaders.

However, as luck would have it, Kanye appeared as a guest on *The Breakfast Club*, a New York-based morning show cohosted by a friend and industry icon, Angela Yee. Angela and I had met years prior when I designed a version of the Air Jordan 2 for Eminem. During our press tour, we visited her at his satellite station, Shady FM, to discuss the story, the positioning, and the excitement around the highly anticipated product.

Due to our friendship, Angela contacted me directly to verify if what Kanye had shared was true.

"Kanye said you left Nike. Is that true? Hit me back. I know you don't like your business out there like that."

Kanye announced his departure from Nike live on their show, mentioning my name during the early morning hours in New York. Unfortunately, due to the time difference, I was asleep and unable to respond to her in time to provide my side of the story.

My first thought was, *Who told him I was leaving?*

As the news of my departure spread among the ranks, I received many calls and texts to verify how I knew Kanye and if I was genuinely resigning from Nike.

God's grace gave me the foresight to share my plans with Phil Knight, the chairman and founder of Nike; Larry Miller, the president of Jordan Brand; and John Hoke, Nike's chief design officer, days before the news of our affiliation was made public.

They graciously offered to help me transition from the company into my position as a full-time father.

While everyone else was joining the witch hunt to besmirch my name, they held steadfast, offering words of support and pushing back colleagues who questioned my timing.

Despite the accusations and ridicule, I concluded all work with Jordan and planned for our next chapter.

My mission to create gadgets for my heroes had ended, and a new mission was emerging.

I wanted to build stronger children rather than fix broken adults.

The power of prevention had superseded the profitable notion of correction. So I reclaimed my gifts from corporate America and centered my efforts on my son.

We were at peace with our decision. We chose the path that forced us to rely solely on the grace and majesty of God alone.

We were free, but as we soon learned, freedom came with a price.

CHAPTER 15

WELCOME TO TRILLICON VALLEY

If necessity is the mother of invention, then determination must be the father of innovation.

Leaving any job while you are the sole provider for your family is hard.

I believe the role of a parent is to be a steward of their children, not an overseer. This reframing of parental strategy in the context of Black family dynamics was in contrast to the popular narrative. So often, Black fathers were regarded as absent, oppressed, or abusive. Never shown with a range of emotions and intellect, the idea of an involved Black father—equal parts caregiver and breadwinner—was disregarded as a myth.

So it came as no surprise to me when my former colleagues spread rumors about what they perceived was the "true" reason for my departure.

"He's going to Adidas to work with Kanye."

"He's a traitor. I heard he got caught stealing shoes and selling them on eBay."

"Man, how can he afford to quit? I mean, it's not like he's wealthy. Something must be up."

Every time someone shared a comment with me, I felt more betrayed. Thankfully, close friends who remained at Nike frequently defended my name and character when former colleagues questioned my intentions.

Those who knew me understood the reason for my departure. My family was the center of every decision I made throughout my career. The accusations of how I was creating an imaginary crisis to work with Kanye were in tremendous conflict with my character and their firsthand experience with me as a person and professional.

Rumors and veiled threats of litigation continued for months. Meanwhile, I had negotiated with Stanford to return to campus as a fellow at the Hasso Plattner Institute of Design, a.k.a. the d.school. My friend and former professor, Dr. Jennifer Aaker, and Chris Flink, an IDEO design executive at the time, had been in close contact with me throughout the year and were helping me think through my next steps.

They were preparing a plan to bring me back to Stanford in a capacity that would allow me to research ways to help my son while reestablishing my presence in Silicon Valley. We committed to leaving our childhood dreams and stepping into our adult responsibilities. My wife and I made every decision with love and deep introspection.

Eventually, the controversy of my unexpected departure shifted toward public displays of compassion and support. My former colleagues soon realized I was on a path that prioritized my family above all. Finally, I knew I was the man I had claimed to be.

Immediately after I arrived at the d.school, the news of my presence garnered the attention of curious students eager to hear more of my story after attending TEDx Stanford the previous year.

My faculty position provided me with diverse professional interactions and academic insight. In addition, my story piqued the interest of companies like Google, SAP, and Disney, which had inquired about securing me as a guest speaker on the topics of purpose and design.

As I immersed myself in the program, I began exploring various value-creation paths while simultaneously working with doctors to discover the cause of my son's rapid weight gain.

We eventually discovered he had a small tear in his lower intestine, which had led to severe inflammation. Finally, we had an answer, and now we could figure out a solution to build up the lining of his intestinal wall and his confidence, identity, and self-efficacy. The journey had worn us all down, and we finally saw the light at the end of the tunnel.

Our response was swift and effective. According to our research and with the guidance of our medical advisors, our best course of action would be to remove everything from his diet and slowly add things back one by one to see what triggered a reaction. Eventually, we discovered increasing his collagen intake, reducing acidic foods, and providing consistent encouragement would help him heal.

Unfortunately, the lasting impact of his torn intestinal wall caused him to develop insulin resistance. As a result, he could not enjoy the small delights of childhood. When other children had birthday parties and unlimited access to various foods, our son had to read labels, monitor his intake, and mentally prepare to explain why he could not enjoy the things his classmates could. We saw these as healthy habits that would bring him a balanced and healthy lifestyle as an adult. The short-term impact was worth the long-term gain.

We were well on the road to healing our son and our family unit. But we wanted to help other children struggling with similar emotional, physiological, and behavioral impediments. My mind swirled with ideas.

Should I start a nonprofit, a company, or a movement?

Until that point, I had never experienced professional failure. As a result, I was hesitant to jump directly into building my own company. Business school had prepared me for the reality of creating a start-up. However, failure was and always will be a possible outcome.

I knew my weaknesses and professional gaps, and I set out to strategically acquire the skill sets and insights to create my own venture-backed company. My process was simple: expand my network to expand my knowledge.

Moving back to Silicon Valley required me to shift from creating soft goods to software. My time in Digital Sport provided me with a growing network of founders, investors, and technologists. From my research, my initial idea was called "The Tribe," and its mission was to create a modern evolution of the Boy Scouts. I wondered how to reach at-risk middle-school-age Black and Latino boys through exploration and adventure.

I researched, designed, and created prototypes for several experiences that exposed young men to different forms of success and mental resilience. The culminating prototype was a daylong event held at the d.school that highlighted the challenges and the mindsets of victorious Black and Latino men.

Despite the success of my prototype, I still needed more experience to form a company. So I paused work and decided to learn by doing. I joined numerous start-ups in various categories to understand their early challenges.

After making this crucial ideological shift, I immediately realized I needed to expand my knowledge network. I was now in the presence of influential Stanford alumni, and I wanted to learn as much as I could as fast as I could. As a result, opportunities poured in from start-ups, established companies, and curious venture capitalists connected to Stanford. Over the next few months, I devised a clear plan that would allow me to evolve into a designer-founder focused on children's well-being.

I broke the process into three phases: join a start-up, join a start-up as a cofounder, and finally, start a company and find other cofounders.

Naturally, joining a start-up involved interviews with founders who often used their grand vision to emphasize the opportunity they had discovered. This tactic would allow them to convince highly skilled candidates to accept compensation as equity in the company rather than a traditional cash-based salary.

By providing equity, founders preserved the cash they had in the bank to reinvest into the product, service, or experience. In the case of Mark One, the first company I joined, we provided a physical hardware product and a mobile app experience, each with its own set of complexities. The company eventually dissolved into a shell of its founder's vision.

Here is what I learned along the way:

1. **How a venture capitalist treats a founder during a down cycle is genuinely who they are.**

I had never raised capital before, so I observed how the founder prepared to share bad news with the board, which consisted of investors and strategic advisors. When the CEO of Mark One delivered the information, I noticed a shift in tone from our investors and a firm emphasis on finding a near-term solution that did not require more of their capital. Each investor had a limited amount of time, so they did not make decisions based on emotion. They only had time for businesses with early success indicators, known as "product market fit." The more your audience consumes your product, the more attractive you become to potential investors. Money flowed toward founders who did not need it due to the perception of their success. Naturally, this behavior incentivized founders to inflate their financial projections and product development milestones. As such, most first-time founders tended to downplay the difficulties of building their vision. After watching the CEO get scolded for not sharing terrible news sooner, I knew investors offered patience to honest and proactive founders, not liars and procrastinators. Professional maturity is a crucial indicator of potential success for a prudent investor.

2. **Refrain from preparing to receive a yes from a customer or investor. Seek instead to eliminate the ways that would lead to a no.**

Introspection and self-awareness are crucial to building a company. Identifying inefficiencies in your leadership style, business model, and product reduces your risk of missing critical signals for when a behavior should be scaled or discarded. In addition, when you practice introspection consistently, you remove the elements of your idea that do not entice your intended target audiences to take action.

3. **Hire people who are more intelligent than you and let them add value.**

Simply put, there is no such thing as a "lone genius." Some first-time founders view praise assigned to other employees as an assault on their intellect. The stories of a person toiling away in their garage for countless hours before discovering their billion-dollar idea distort inexperienced new founders ability to share the glory with their team. I learned my job was to share the praise with the team when things were going well. My job was also to receive the blame when things went awry.

Mark One ultimately shut down, and shortly after, prolific investor Ryan Sweeney recruited me to Accel Partners, a prominent venture capital firm in Silicon Valley.

Ryan was a collegiate athlete with a deep love for footwear culture. He was eager to bring design closer to the venture capital world. In 2015, this was a unique position for a large firm. Only one other firm at the time, Kleiner Perkins Caufield Byers (KPCB), had the foresight to leverage design as a critical contributor to their fund's thesis. John Maeda—the former leader of MIT's prestigious Media Lab and a brilliant educator, designer, and futurist—guided and mentored me when I accepted the role at Accel.

John was the first design partner at a significant firm in the Valley, and he reached out to share his experience with me. He cared deeply about improving the opportunity landscape for designers, which showed in his consistent advocacy.

The role of designer-in-residence allowed me to merge my creative and operational aspirations while maintaining my academic post at Stanford. It was the best of both worlds.

As the contract period ended with the d.school, a medical revelation devastated my world again. My father had been diagnosed with bladder cancer and needed immediate treatment.

I was committed to using my gifts and talents for the purposes God placed on my heart. I wanted to walk a narrow path that would eventually lead to creating a family-based company that directly impacted the lives of children. I wanted to spend time with my father and do work that fostered a deeper connection to my own children.

My next adventure required a new creative expression vehicle. At this moment, Trillicon Valley was born. I was not trying to pick a lane; I was determined to create my own. My lectures had taken me around the world, and I needed a way to signal to others something new was being born in the heart of Silicon Valley, a movement grounded in the universal principles of honor and gratitude. I remained part-time faculty at the d.school for several months while I transitioned to Accel.

At Accel, I learned the intricacies of venture capital and the nuanced investment process. While I was there, a former Nike colleague, Bryant Barr, who had recently gained acceptance to the Stanford Graduate School of Business, contacted me about a business idea. He and I formed a friendship on the basketball court during morning runs with Nike's finance and operations executives. The 6:00 a.m. run was more about brokering relationships, discussing outside investment activities, and navigating the complexities of business. As a designer with a business degree, I found our conversations refreshing. Moreover, it led to relationships with other ambitious young leaders.

This bond continued into the entrepreneurship space. Though I started in an advisory role, Bryant and I cofounded Slyce, a mobile platform for influencers and athletes to manage the various requirements of posting on social media, alongside Stephen Curry, who had recently skyrocketed to the top of elite sports. His style of play, faith in God, and loyalty to his friends allowed us to create something that would bring efficiency to his life and others' lives—anyone who carried the weight of influence.

For the next eighteen months, we traveled the continent meeting with partners such as Under Armour and led consumer-facing events for the 2016 NBA All-Star Weekend in Toronto.

As a result of a failed round of funding, I would eventually leave to pursue my purpose again.

By cofounding Slyce while working for Accel, I learned the following two things:

1. **Investors bet on founding teams, not their idea.** Over time, ideas tend to shift due to market conditions, technical challenges, or product readiness. Great teams anticipate change and thrive in ambiguity.

2. **After a while, no one cares about the "romance." They want results.** Great storytellers can secure initial rounds of capital to start a company. However, great operators guarantee growth through revenue and additional funding rounds to scale a company. Great storytellers and great operators are often two different people.

My time at Slyce ended, and I was again on the path toward creating my own company. I had experienced a full range of start-up failure, loss, dysfunction, and a healthy dose of comedic relief from comparing characters from the show *Silicon Valley* to people I had interacted with in real life.

If necessity is the mother of invention, then determination must be the father of innovation.

While seeking information to spark my imagination, I stumbled upon the work of Joseph Campbell, a visionary mythology scholar and literature professor. Campbell's *The Hero with a Thousand Faces* is a nonfiction work that presents his theory of the "monomyth," or the narrative tropes that form the foundation of traditional storytelling.

I discovered the science of heroism and was eager to apply my learnings to my next venture.

The time had come for me to rise and create with conviction. My love for my family inspired me to create something to impact the lives of children worldwide.

My destiny had finally arrived.

CHAPTER 16

DESERT OF NEGEV

Faith requires bravery in the presence of the unknown.

After diving into the depths of Joseph Campbell's work, I searched for additional academic scholarship that chronicled the power and impact of the hero archetype in modern society. My query led me to empirical evidence of the importance of the labels we use to describe ourselves and how those labels impact our cognitive and emotional development.

The "Batman effect" proves that when elementary-aged schoolchildren adopt an alter ego, an extreme form of "self-distancing," they can effectively observe their feelings objectively and view a difficult situation more dispassionately. Children who impersonated an exemplar other, in this case, a character such as Batman, spent the most time working (White et. al 2016).

By believing they were superheroes, children were biased toward their "exemplar self," the "super" version of themselves accessible through their imagination. Their enhanced efficacy was a familiar phenomenon in my previous career. By wearing the uniform of our heroes, we often believed we could "Be Like Mike." I immediately knew I needed to create a multimodal system of play that leveraged characters, physical products, and narrative-based play experiences.

The mission was simple: "Entertain, delight, and surprise every child in the world through imaginative and interactive play." We needed to become a brand of "first," supremely confident with a simple, soulful, fun, and fearless market position that captivated the mind of every child. Play would become prevention to build stronger children.

Earlier in the year, Ryan Smith, a fellow Stanford alum from the south side of Chicago, introduced me to Earvin "Magic" Johnson. Ryan was leading Johnson's foray into venture investing and was curious about my plans to build a brand. With divine provocation, Ryan recommended I meet them at a gala dinner in Chicago where I was honored for my commitment to pursuing fair and equitable treatment of Black and Brown children in the education system.

After delivering my keynote address, I was bombarded with requests to connect with educators, students, and prominent political figures. Attendees, such as former Secretary of Education Arne Duncan, offered support, while others offered start-up capital and operational resources. I was overwhelmed with an abundance of love and appreciation.

Johnson, however, saw beyond the surface of my appeal. He felt a deeper connection to my mission, and he left the event believing one day I would start my own company, and when that day came, he would be one of the first to invest.

Months later, I prepared to raise my first official round of capital. After months of market research, I settled on a name, position, and mission for my company.

Super Heroic, the world's first company focused on multimodal play, was created to solve the rising obesity epidemic and mental health crisis that plagued elementary-school-age children. By leveraging our knowledge of product development, science-backed narratives, and physical play, we could improve the health of children all over the world.

I had successfully created early prototypes and secured product development and manufacturing resources in Asia while caring for my parents, who arrived in Palo Alto to begin my father's chemotherapy treatments at Stanford Hospital.

I was overwhelmed with the weight of starting a company during familial uncertainty.

Sonny and I buckled down; I increased the frequency of my speaking engagements while maintaining my position at Accel and methodically leveraging our life savings to establish Super Heroic as an incorporated entity.

Finally, in October 2016, Super Heroic received its first official investment round from John Maeda; Pierre Omidyar, the founder of eBay; Accel; and my wife's uncle Maurice Duca, a fellow Stanford alum and founder of Investment Group Santa Barbra.

As things progressed, my cofounders, Harshal Sisodia and Devaris Brown, and I discussed the importance of having someone on the team who would focus solely on operations and supply chain, an area of expertise perfectly aligned with my father's skill set. While battling cancer, he continued to consult with companies. He loved the feeling of solving complex problems for product-based organizations.

My father joining Super Heroic was the perfect scenario. Finally, I would be able to spend every waking moment with my father, building a company inspired by my son, his grandson, while supporting his healing journey.

We kept the news of his cancer a secret from the team and our investors. As a result, no one knew what we were fighting emotionally. We remained steadfast in our mission and never shared the depth of our familial struggle.

Over the years, we strengthened our team with the addition of Estelle Maranan, the former head of footwear development for Jordan and Curry brands; Sylvester Peoples, the former merchandising director at Nike; Ron Mead, a young designer from Los Angeles; and Shirley Yau, a finance and operations lead from New York.

Additionally, we successfully obtained funding rounds from Playground Global, Magic Johnson, and Foot Locker, which allowed us to launch the brand, secure global distribution, and break new ground in the children's market segments.

Our work was heralded as innovative and disruptive. As a result, we won a Red Dot award for Design Excellence, an Edison Genius Award, a Fast Company Design Excellence Award, and two official "Super Heroic Day" proclamations in Stockton, California, and East Palo Alto, California, respectively.

Fun Fact: I was given my own day in Austin, Texas. March 17 is the official "Jason Mayden Day" during the creative ideas-based festival South by Southwest (SXSW).

Partnerships with Nickelodeon, Nerf, and NASA allowed us to pierce culture with a provocative position that contrasted from my peers 'work and focus. In addition, my choice to dedicate my gifts and talents to the youth positioned me as a leading voice in childhood development, creativity, and play-based industries.

Everyone around me lived in their purpose, and our collective energy manifested our wildest dreams. By this time, my parents were fully settled in the Bay Area, and our routine had evolved. In addition, my mentee and close friend, Jordan Simmons, had recently graduated from USC and landed a position with the Oakland Raiders as an undrafted rookie. While at USC, I served as a mentor and big brother, helping him navigate the complexities of being a student athlete with aspirations of being an entrepreneur. He lived with us during his rookie year. We were both rookies to some extent. He was fighting for a position in the NFL, and I was fighting for a position in the market. We were rising as one.

Life propelled us forward, and we relocated Super Heroic from Palo Alto to East Oakland. Our headquarters were affectionately known as the "Hero Lab." Each element of the office had a hidden meaning, from a table that doubled as a swing set to a small rock-climbing wall against the silhouette of a cityscape. We created our own world in our own way.

However, this dream came with a cost. My physical and mental health suffered as I traveled across the country, pitching investors, giving lectures, and securing partnerships with companies such as Foot Locker, Nickelodeon, and Hasbro. For the last four years, I carried the weight of being a deeply committed father, husband, friend, and son. I worked two to three jobs at a time to ensure we had the financial resources to support the healing of my father, my children's varied academic interests, and my wife's sustained well-being. I was heading rapidly toward a dangerous place of depression and fatigue. I needed to rest but did not have the luxury.

I had no safety net. God was my plan A, and I was plan B.

I was lost and searching for an answer I could only find through deep prayer, meditation, and supplication.

The further I pushed myself to the edge of my abilities, the more God's grace fell upon me. I was his, and he was revealing himself in unimaginable ways.

In the summer of 2019, I was invited to visit Israel as part of a program funded by the Charles and Lynn Schusterman Family Philanthropies. This global organization seeks to improve lives, strengthen communities, and advance equity. They believe in the power of curating groups of individuals under the principle of Judaism known as *tikkun olam*, which can be defined as any activity that heals the world.

I felt called to visit Israel.

My mother's mixed ethnicity was obvious by her complexion and hair texture. However, not until my siblings and I became adults did we discover her father was an Ashkenazi Jew who committed adultery with my grandmother while in a relationship with another woman. This unknown part of my heritage left a gaping hole in my identity. I was a displaced indigenous Black man and a descendant of an absent Jewish grandfather.

Gathering my emotions, I set out with the desire to encounter God. I needed to see with my own eyes the locations of significance that form the basis of my faith. I wanted to see, experience, and feel the healing grace of God's everlasting love.

My heart was ready to receive healing. The work I had done in therapy revealed where trauma resided in my soul.

I was breaking free of my toxic ambition. I needed to be seen and accepted by a world that often ridiculed and rejected people who did not fit neatly into distorted, monolithic constructs. I arrived in Israel with one question: "Does God love me?"

As I searched for God's essence in each moment, I found myself wandering Jerusalem's streets, led by a spirit of curiosity that placed me at the threshold of one of the holy city's oldest businesses—an antique shop. Much like the glass shop in Paulo Coelho's masterpiece *The Alchemist*, the revelation that God wrote everything before time took me aback.

The antique shop owner spoke about his time as a visiting professor at the Art Institute of Chicago, the place where I advanced my skills while doing my undergrad at CCS. He shared countless stories of Jerusalem's mysterious ability to normalize events other contexts would view as miracles and how everyone who came with a desire to hear from God ultimately did. I listened intently to his every word, wondering if

I would have my moment with God. I shared how my mother inspired my desire to reclaim a heritage lost to time. She had only experienced life as a Black woman, as she was never allowed to build a meaningful relationship with her biological father.

My honest desire to heal moved him, and he urged me to continue my quest. Then, as I turned to leave, he grabbed my arm and smiled with the warmth of a friend.

"I don't know if this means anything to you, but I wanted to tell you this. I have this overwhelming feeling to tell you God does love you. More than you know."

I immediately burst into tears. I had not shared my prayer with anyone on the trip. Days prior, while visiting the shores of the Sea of Galilee at dawn, I closed my eyes and asked God for forgiveness for my transgressions. I was hurting deeply, and I needed to know if he loved me. I needed his grace now more than ever.

I felt the power of God's presence at that moment, and it transformed me.

As the trip ended, we visited the desert of Negev, a location that carried the aggregated energy of every living being that ever existed. The magnetic essence of standing in one of civilization's most traveled paths eclipses any experience I had to date. Standing under the stars among the world's most prolific creatives, I prayed to God, thanking him for the love and abundance he provided me my entire life. I called on my ancestors' strength and prayed over our progeny's well-being.

I was performing for an audience of one. So I rejoiced for God and God alone.

Upon the conclusion of my open plea, my peers surrounded me and began to cry as they felt the Spirit overtake our group. We all felt something beyond this realm that bonded us together for life. We all felt the pure, unconditional, eternal *agape* type of love.

My body was tired and my mind was overwhelmed with anxiety, but my soul was at peace. I was in deep communion with the Holy Spirit after my intercession with God on destiny's winding road. After returning from Israel, I was immediately pulled back into the rigorous routine of lecturing, fundraising, and promoting Super Heroic's vision. As 2019 closed, I fell ill while visiting Foot Locker's headquarters in New York. A Super Heroic investor based in Shanghai, China, had told me a severe flu was causing disruptions to manufacturing resources in Asia. The urgency in his message was alarming.

"Jason, have you heard about the shutdown in China? Has that affected you at all? What's your plan if you can't produce the product in time?"

His barrage of questions brought on an anxiety attack as I sat alone in my hotel room in New York, preparing to return home to Chicago to speak to the staff of the first Foot Locker that provided me with a safe harbor after my traumatic experience. His noticeable tone of concern caused me to contact several of my former Stanford classmates who resided in China and had also invested in Super Heroic. They confirmed their country's supply chain disruptions.

I fell to my knees, begging God to release me from my pain and sorrow. I knew this chapter of my life was coming to an abrupt end.

Super Heroic had met an unnamed, insurmountable foe.

In only a matter of time, the entire world would come to a standstill.

Looking back, God gave me the foresight to pursue a more ethical path. I chose to stop attempting to persuade investors to fund a business that was inevitably being forced to close due to a tariff war and a global pandemic.

What felt like punishment was preparation for a redistribution of grace into the parts of my life left unattended in my pursuit of material gain.

CHAPTER 17

THE PRESENT HELP

A profound sense of loss, hope, and joy is the inevitable outcome of chasing the wind.

Creatio ex nihilo, or "create out of nothing" in Latin, is my creed. Being a cultural cultivator (new word alert) requires each element of my life to become my teacher as I praise those who assist me in bringing my dreams to fruition. However, as a leader, I also receive the blame for the failings of those I steward. They are only as good as the instruction, mentorship, and resources I supplied to complete the task.

Creative leadership requires much more than provocative speech and persuasive ideas. It begs the creative to look within. Introspection serves as the primary method of cultivation in the process of creating culture. Inconvenience is our muse. Difficulty brings about a sense of ingenuity.

Too often, we conflate leadership with power, power with wealth, and wealth with altruistic intent. In the context of grace and creativity, leadership is self-discipline and restraint. It is a visceral dedication to doing the inconvenient and exceptionally difficult thing for the betterment of the collective.

The job of a cultural cultivator exists beyond time and circumstance. We boldly lean into new ways of thinking and expressing ourselves. Unfortunately, this often leads to frustration rather than joy. It does not feel good to see what others have yet to discover. The mind questions whether you are either born in the wrong era or have a perspective only a select few can understand.

Each interaction with your creative peers only furthers your hunger to discover the undone and push the boundaries of your imagination's exploration. It's an overwhelming feeling that comes with introducing a new vibration into the current creative flow of humanity. Your inner child is unbound. It's euphoric.

My humble assumption is, if you are reading this, you are a cultivator pursuing the unknown. I too have been urged to seek the unimaginable heights of being unapologetically me, in public, on purpose, all the time.

"No one will understand this. Simplify your idea. It's just too out there." These are the rationalized thoughts of a defeatist who has not always felt seen. However, revealing your weakness also welcomes your strength to present itself urgently at the edge of your identity. Simply put, one cannot conquer what one does not confront. Pursuing more, I have leaned into failure and embraced its bittersweet lessons.

My inconvenient thing revealed itself in a moment of despair.

In October 2019, I was coming down from my professional high and feeling lost and depleted in the same way an elite sprinter would at the end of a race where they did not perform to their expectations. From my first major entrepreneurial endeavor emerged the staggering presence of imminent failure. My intrinsic behaviors, emotions, and predisposed response mechanisms to external threats no longer pleased my ego. Instead, they all began to plague my soul. Anger and insecurity replaced the sustenance of achievement my ego feasted on freely my entire career. Accomplishment became addictive and no longer served as a form of self-worth.

I was caught in the late-stage throws of founder's fatigue, that desperate feeling of exhaustion and anxiety. It's a stress-induced free fall from the heights of starting a new endeavor to the depths of emotional, physical, and often mental debilitation. Failure destroyed my confidence in my abilities. All I could do was cling to the fading thoughts of when I felt most aligned with God's love for me. His present help kept me calm as I faced what I thought was my last battle with my insatiable desire to succeed rather than to do things based on a desire to please God.

As luck would have it, upon leaving a leadership training program my former Stanford professor Dr. Carole Robin had founded, I found myself failing at the thing I was being taught to do.

I was not just battling the daily struggles of being a founder but also dealing with intergenerational trauma that bubbled to the surface after years of being suppressed behind the mask of success.

As Black children, we are told to get half as far, we need to work twice as hard. This means to be viewed as equal in a professional setting, our effort would need to be *four times* that of a white peer of similar competence and ability.

Extrapolating this concept further would mean we require *sixteen times* the effort to be regarded as excellent and *two hundred and fifty-six times* the effort to be considered exceptional within our chosen vocation. This toxic ideology misleads us to believe that working harder is the path toward generational wealth and sovereignty. Unfortunately, the sadistic "hustle porn" narrative that fuels today's creative industry has persuaded us to trade well-being for well-doing—to our harm.

It's impossible to outwork a system designed to profit from self-deprecation and neglect. From the outset, I realized there could never be an equal and balanced way to measure our efforts to be seen as capable and qualified. The variables for marginalized communities are ever-changing and offer infinite outcomes corporate America can never address by focusing on inclusion within the workplace.

My failed attempt at introspection, brought about by an anxiety attack, convinced me my heart was beating beyond my ability to soothe my pain. I rushed to urgent care where I was subjected to a battery of tests to rule out cardiac arrest as the root of my pain.

I lay there contemplating my choices: Should I have left a stable job? What happens to my legacy, my family, and my ideas? *Will* anyone remember and understand what I stood for? Each thought rushed to the forefront of my mind. But then, I decided I did not want to succumb to the weight of the insane pressure I placed on myself.

As the doctor approached, I braced myself for the worst. He opened his mouth. Time seemed to stand still. He asked me why I was doing this to myself.

"Is the company worth your life?"

I was relieved I was only having a panic attack but was scared because it had felt so *extreme*. He was right. Why *was* I doing this to myself? What began as a dream to inspire my son had become my Achilles' heel.

Searching for answers, I felt an overwhelming urge to write a creative direction for my life. I rebelled against the modern concept of time and linear output. Instead of focusing on what I wanted to accomplish by Friday, I would focus on how I wanted to feel by Friday. I had evolved from *chronos*, chronological time, to *kairos*, God's time—the opportune time to take action.

Below is the basic framework I created for myself. Use it as a catalyst for replenishment and repair. Use it as a first step toward healing from founder's fatigue, a creative block, or an overall feeling of being burned out. We can all relate to that feeling at some point in our lives. I am no different. I just utilized my skills to create a way from nothing, much like God has done for me time and time again.

Super Heroic was ending, but a new adventure was emerging. This one would bring me even closer to my purpose. This adventure would lead me to seek help and finally heal.

JASON MAYDEN: PERSONAL AND PROFESSIONAL RESTORATION DESIGN STRATEGY

MY ANCHOR SCRIPTURES

Ephesians 5:15–16

"Be very careful, then, how you live—not as unwise but as wise, making the most of every opportunity, because the days are evil."

1 Corinthians 6:19–20

"Do you not know that your bodies are temples of the Holy Spirit, who is in you, whom you have received from God? You are not your own; you were bought at a price. Therefore honor God with your bodies."

PERSONAL CREATIVE DIRECTION

Metamorphosis: My evolution, fueled by a desire to live based on qualitative time (kairos) instead of quantitative time (chronos).

COACHING ETHOS

Financial Coach: Wealth is behavior and mindset, *not* a number. Master the behaviors of wealth.

Combat Sports Coach: The most effective form of wealth is health. Self-care is not selfish. It's essential.

Naturopathic/Medical Coach: God has given us all we need. Food is medicine. A diet consists of what you ingest both physically and cognitively. Be mindful of what you allow into your body.

Science is artistry and logic combined. Be sure to understand and measure every incremental point of your health. We cannot improve what we do not measure.

Mental Performance Coach: Your greatest enemy is your "inner me." Be mindful of your inner dialogue. Learn to speak kindly to yourself.

Executive Coach: Leadership is a learned behavior, not a title. If you are a leader and no one is following you, you're just a person taking a walk. Learn how to communicate effectively by setting clear, measurable goals for yourself and your team.

WHAT I NEED FROM MY COACHES

1. Clear, actionable plans
2. Clear, efficient communication
3. Help to set KPIs for my personal success

WHAT MY COACHES NEED FROM ME

1. Trust
2. Respect
3. Clear, direct communication

KEY PERSONAL OBSERVATIONS

What behaviors, feelings, and emotions do not serve my highest good?

- Lack of energy
- Anxiety
- Low morale
- Constant worry
- Overwhelm

- Difficulty saying "no" to people
- Lack of time to learn what is needed to grow
- Lack of motivation for physical activity
- Early/middle stages of founder's fatigue

DEFINE MY "PROBLEM STATEMENT"

How might I prioritize well-being over well-doing?

SOLUTION IDEATION

- Create a wellness-based calendar.
- Change mindset from "How much can I get done by Friday?" to "How do I want to feel by Friday?"
- Establish a strict in-person/online meeting amount policy:
  - Any meeting less than an hour should be a phone call or a Zoom.
  - Do not accept more than three one-hour-long Zoom or in-person meetings per week.
- Delegate with courage. I do not need to be everywhere for everything.

STRICT MEETING FILTERS

- Clearly define reasons for meeting.
- Ruthlessly edit the attendee list. Do not feel compelled to invite everyone. Recaps are fine.
- Have a values-plus-priority decision schema.
- Define whether the decision is personal, brand, or margin accretive.
- Clearly state the desired outcome.
- Plan for things to go wrong and prioritize the things that lessen or mitigate risk.
- Always do what's right, even when no one is looking.
- Be kind to yourself. Never make decisions when angry, tired, stressed, or hungry—especially hungry.

BUSINESS AND PERSONAL PRIORITIES

1. My well-being
2. Improve communication
3. Restoration
4. Time management

ORDER OF IMPORTANCE

1. God
2. Me
3. My immediate family
4. Team
5. Board
6. Investors
7. Key partners

CLEARLY DEFINE ORGANIZATIONAL PLAN WITH KEY ROLES AND OBJECTIVES

1. Simplified operating model plus strategic plan
2. Manage burn
3. Growth: size of audience plus top-line revenue

ESTABLISH CRITICAL KPIS THAT MATTER FOR SERIES A (REFERENCE SERIES B)

- Inventory churn
- Burn rate
- Customer acquisition cost (CAC)
- Return on ad spend (ROAS)
- Conversions
- Lifetime value (LTV)
- Operational expenditure (OPEX)
- Monthly and annually recurring revenue (MRR/ARR)

CHAPTER 18

JEHOVAH JIREH

Change is inevitable. Growth is optional.

In the Black community, seeking help for intergenerational trauma is often considered a sign of weakness. However, admitting my limitations required me to expose my vulnerability and insecurity.

My entire life, I suppressed feelings of despair that lingered in the shadows of my subconscious. However, failing at what I believed was my purpose brought profound depression and embarrassment.

In 2020, the world froze with news of a virulent biological threat to humanity, and the virus, COVID-19, would add significant complexity to a hectic time in global trade relations.

Exorbitant tariffs, rising xenophobic rhetoric, and fear-mongering amid law enforcement's sustained violence against Black communities created a total erasure of civility in society. As a result, we devolved toward an authoritarian state.

Daily calls from lawyers, investors, liquidators, and employees filled my heart with angst. We decided to dissolve the company.

Our product was not allowed to be released from customs, and the Chinese government froze our supply chain indefinitely. The composition of my investors and team would not allow me to pivot to another business model. My choices were limited, and the apparent path forward required immense personal and financial sacrifice.

My wife and I decided to continue paying for the expenses of employees who remained a part of Super Heroic while they were searching for new employment. As a result, our resources were depleted, but our hearts were full.

Despite our loss, we provided food, clothing, and supplies to people in an unhoused encampment in Echo Park, California. God compelled us to serve alongside a friend, Talia Caldwell, who had made it her mission to care for the most vulnerable people during the early days of the pandemic.

The year progressed, and as a nation, we fell deeper into civil unrest and societal upheaval. The pandemic fractured our willingness to assemble in person. We vacated the foundational institutions we once frequented as people retreated to their homes to seek safety from enemies known and imagined.

I continued my therapy over Zoom, feeling more engaged in my healing process. I was transitioning from an observer of my pain to a participant in my inner peace. With my newfound calm, I shifted my lecturing and teaching online.

My virtual course, Shoe and Tell, was designed to demystify the world of collaborations between influencers, athletes, and global brands. The free class provided students an escape from the dire emotion of our present circumstances, and hopefully a respite from the collective trauma we were and are enduring. Despite our financial struggle, we continued to serve and give.

Leaning on the gifts and wisdom of my peers, I contacted NBA superstar Chris Paul, WNBA legend Chiney Ogwumike, and iconic designer Jerry Lorenzo, who I met backstage on the first leg of Kanye's Yeezus tour in Seattle in 2013.

Their selfless participation in the Shoe and Tell series offered me much-needed excitement during a time of sadness. This experience reignited my desire to help my friends achieve their dreams while I waited on God to reveal the next step in my journey.

By March 2020, the world shifted entirely to remote work while most people fiercely protected any semblance of normalcy. My friend and the former editor of *Complex*, Gerald Flores, saw my efforts to uplift the spirit of the culture, and God compelled him to reach out and connect with me to establish a weekly Bible study. There, we welcomed anyone searching for community during this period of isolation. We began to videoconference every Saturday, welcoming more and more members who had shared the news of our impromptu virtual study group.

After my class concluded, Jerry Lorenzo and I remained in close contact. His brand, Fear of God, had become dominant in fashion, and as his partnership with Nike ended, we discussed the idea of joining forces to create an athletic pillar of his business. We believed in the power of community and shared a desire to provide hope and aspiration to an industry in need of a revolution. We spoke with every suitor, praying for clarity as we navigated opportunities that would provide significant economic rewards and meaningful benefits to the culture. We sought a partner who saw us as business leaders capable of leading an organization through a radical brand transformation. We chose to be deployed by God and not employed by man.

Our informal conversations progressed into advanced discussions with Adidas. They were courting us with the promise of overseeing the basketball division, a category that Adidas had significantly underserved in North America.

Nike and Jordan's market dominance in that segment had made it quite difficult for anyone to capture new value. It would take the combined knowledge of a self-taught, talented luxury designer and a curious, creative innovator to invent something radically new. However, God had brought us together in an irrefutable way. We had the experience, understanding of culture, and relevant skills to provide energy and inspiration to Adidas at the right time.

Jerry and I began a radical shift in athletic luxury through the elegance and effortless versatility of Fear of God's aesthetic.

In December 2020, we announced the formation of Fear of God Athletics to critical acclaim. I would join the company as its first employee in the capacity of president. My character and reputation provided my family with economic opportunities to sustain our well-being during a difficult period of loss and grief. Working for an organization that glorified and revered the omnipresent grace of God was an honor and privilege and in complete alignment with my journey.

Trillicon Valley and its global community of artists, athletes, technologists, activists, investors, and entrepreneurs continued to provide value worldwide through advocacy and access.

Our position placed us at the table of some of the most transformative deals in culture. For years, I worked behind the scenes, helping to design strategies, creative direction, and deal points for influential athletes, designers, and entertainers. I fought to protect their creative visions and integrity. Finally, my time arrived to reap the benefits of my quiet efforts to protect Black creativity.

Life accelerated immediately. My children had overcome the initial frustrations and complications of attending virtual school. Nevertheless, they missed formative rites of passage typical teenagers enjoy. Birthdays came and went, and we remained, sheltered in place, longing to return to normalcy.

My wife and I attended therapy together. We wanted to provide a place of peace and growth for one another. Unfortunately, remaining still forced us to confront the impact of our childhood trauma. The dynamic nature of our parental duties provided us with a convenient distraction. We replaced introspection with oversight of our children's development. We could no longer outrun our childhood pain. So we chose to heal.

The beginning of my journey started with a brokenhearted child's act of desperation. After that, I experienced rejection, participated in rebellion, and found redemption through sacrifice and long-suffering.

I had arrived at my place of purpose.

My story had come full circle once again. I returned to the game I loved as a child while creating opportunities for others to thrive. My previous failure, success, loss, and defeat had given me a more profound empathy for everyone I encountered.

I understood we primarily operate from the perspective of our most tragic experiences. This exposure to threats against our well-being creates our filters for the world. We fuel our inner voice either with love or pain. Each serves as a filter for how we give and receive love.

After years of therapy and enhanced self-care, I overcame depression, found my shine, and accepted I was not intended to race against time.

In my soul, I knew what was meant for me was divinely assigned while I was being formed in my mother's womb.

I only needed to believe in the power of my purpose and juxtapose a world fueled by self-serving agendas and performative altruism.

No longer would I move at the speed of greed.

CHAPTER 19

BEYOND THE VEIL

The mystery and majesty of God's presence are undeniable.

I arrived in Chicago on March 25, 2022. Unfortunately, this would be the last time I would see my grandmother, Barbara Jean Anderson, alive.

My entire life, she told me, "You are a preacher. I know God has chosen you to speak his word. You don't belong in a pulpit, though, baby. Your ministry is in the world." My grandmother had always seen me for what I could be, despite how I viewed myself. We would end each conversation the same way.

"I love you, Grandma."

"I love you more, baby."

She had a way of reminding me she loved me and God loved me. When Grandmother Bootsie passed away, she vowed to fill in the gap. She spent the rest of her life building a deep relationship with her grandchildren and great-grandchildren. So I knew I must return to the place where my story began.

My parents had arrived a few days earlier to assist with transitioning her home from the hospital to her warm, loving home.

Her dying wish was to be among family during her ascension, and we all obliged. Our family loves deeply. Despite living in different states and having competing priorities and tight schedules, the Mayden children descended on her home one final time as the world stood still.

Sounds of laughter and praise greeted everyone as they arrived one by one to honor the Mayden clan's matriarch.

"Oh, it's so good to see you, Jason. Your grandma knew you would come." My twin aunties, Karen and Sharon, always full of glee and life, greeted me as I entered the home.

"Everyone is upstairs. Go on up and get you a plate and say hello."

"Thank you, Auntie," I replied as I climbed the stairs with a heavy heart. It had been a long two years since I last saw my grandmother.

The pandemic had stolen precious time we had to love one another. Our frequent visits transitioned to daily calls during my morning commute.

Memories of our conversations danced across my mind as I entered the kitchen. Her sage advice played like a sweet melody in the corners of my memory reserved for profound moments of love.

She calmed me down when I overthought life decisions with a straightforward phrase: "We see to the corner, but God sees around the corner." These words comforted me in my times of need.

This time, death loomed around the corner, and I was not ready to accept the reality of our changing hierarchy. My parents and aunts were now the family's elders, and that revelation hit my siblings, cousins, and me heavily. We were graduating into the position of our parents, and our children into the place we once held.

Calling my grandmother every day had allowed me to access my childhood. Her voice was comforting and wise, strong and complete.

Fully fed and filled with familiar love, I descended the stairs through the dimly lit passageway and into the narrow corridor that opened up into her basement apartment.

My parents, aunts, and cousins, born and found, stood near the edge of my grandmother's bed, held in the somber embrace of reverence and sadness. Death is a natural part of life; we all knew we were fortunate to have this moment together. During the pandemic, families worldwide were forced to say goodbye to their loved ones over video calls, phone calls, and sometimes only in their silent prayers as they cried themselves to sleep.

We were blessed to be here. God's presence was comforting us beyond words.

I matched each step I took with a deep exhale. Tears of love streamed down my face, dampening the mask that hid my pain. I dared at that moment to face her impending outcome with the same strength she displayed in life.

She was Jonesboro, Arkansas, strong with a south-side-of-Chicago attitude. Not even death could take away her joy.

"Jace, you know your grandma would love you to pray for her," my aunt Sheila said with the certainty of a devout daughter who wanted to honor the wishes of her dying mother.

I stood frozen. I was not an elder; I was not even the most senior grandchild in the room. As a result, the weight and responsibility of praying for my grandmother caused me to ponder if I was worthy of this honorable task.

Eyes closed, heart racing, I began to pray anyway. "Lord, thank you for the opportunity to honor my grandmother. Thank you for the chance to share in the bounty of real love, a love forged in the fire of life's trials and tribulations . . ."

For the next few minutes, I continued to pray earnestly from my heart for a miracle. Each tear watered our spirits. Each word nourished our souls. Then, finally, we stood hand in hand around my grandmother, who lay silently in her bed without visible signs of consciousness.

After my prayer, my aunt Sheila transitioned to singing my grandmother's favorite gospel song. Again, our voices intertwined, sending a harmonic jolt of divine energy into the hearts and minds of everyone within the sound of our voices.

Well, woke up this mo'nin
With my mind, stayin 'on Jesus
Woke up this mo'nin
With my mind, stayin 'on the Lord

Well, woke up this mo'nin
With my mind, stayin 'on Jesus
Halleluh, halleluh, hallelujah

Well, singin 'an 'prayin 'with my mind
Stayin 'on Jesus
Singin 'and playin' with my mind
Stayin 'on the Lord
Singin 'an 'prayin 'with my mind
Stayin' on Jesus
Halleluh, halleluh, hallelujah

The lyrics of my grandmother's favorite hymn "Woke Up This Mornin'" brought us to a place of joy and celebration.

There we stood, in the presence of God's grace, holding hands and honoring the life of Barbara Jean Anderson. My eyes were fixed on every detail of her face. I studied the contours of her eyes, the sheen of her silver hair, and the subtle way she cinched her lips as she exhaled the remnants of life from her lungs.

For a brief moment, my grandmother opened her eyes. Her face displayed the emotions of a daughter seeing the face of her loving father after a long while apart. I knew she was looking beyond the veil of our reality and into the promise of heaven.

I was an attentive audience of one.

She was in awe of God's presence. He had revealed himself to her. I did not need empirical evidence to know she had gazed upon the face of God. Instead, I felt his presence surrounding us.

There I stood, witnessing life beyond the veil of our known reality.

Everything at that moment was perfect and complete.

"Jace, that was beautiful. Just beautiful," Auntie Sheila exclaimed as she walked by me, holding back her tears.

"Thank you, Auntie. I didn't want to mess this up for grandma. I wanted to make her proud."

"Oh baby, you did. *Yes. You. Did.*" Her approval gave me the courage and confidence I needed to stand firm.

I had witnessed something few people would ever experience. It changed me forever. No longer would I pursue opportunities that pulled me away from my ministry. My desire to advocate on behalf of and design for children had lay dormant as a result of Super Heroic's dissolution.

Once again, I was at a pivotal moment in my career. Would I remain a part of Fear of God, or would I fulfill my promise to my grandmother?

The next day, I left Chicago with a heavy heart and a renewed spirit. My assignment was clear. I saw to the corner, but God saw around it.

On March 30, 2022, Barbara Jean Anderson, my beautiful grandmother, ascended to the next plane of existence. She went home where she belonged.

After her passing, my parents decided to return home to California. Enlightened by the experience of being with my grandmother during her final hours, they chose not to remain in Chicago for her public memorial. Our intimate celebration allowed us to find peace and closure as a single-family unit.

Her wish was to be cremated with no open casket and no tears. She was going home to glory, and much like her savior, Yeshua, she was absent from the body and present with the Lord.

The universe conspired to bring me home before her memorial to launch my first book, *A Kid's Book about Design*. My grandmother's provocation persuaded me to double down on my purpose. I continued my silent promise to build stronger children rather than fix broken adults.

On the day of the release, I arrived early to center my thoughts and praise the opportunity to speak life over my city's youth. Semicolon Bookstore served as the backdrop of this significant personal and professional experience. The walls came alive with images of strong, prolific Black literary giants such as James Baldwin and Maya Angelou. The owner, Danielle, a gracefully intelligent and diligent Black founder, gave me an overwhelming reception.

Her presence was comforting. She possessed a similar build, look, and disposition to my grandmother, as if I was spending time with her in an alternate reality. I glanced over at her frequently. I imagined Barbara Jean as a young woman. Full of life and optimism. Opportunity and imagination.

I was right where I was supposed to be at that moment. I had seen beyond the veil of reality and all things were in harmony.

Love abounded as family members, close friends, and mentees arrived alongside a small but highly engaged group from a diverse cross-section of Chicago's creative community.

In my soul, I felt my career, my focus, and my priorities would shift overnight. I knew my time with Fear of God was coming to a close. Adventure beckoned once again.

Life had revealed to me the preciousness of now. The commonly used stoic phrase *momento mori*, translated as "remember you will die," catalyzed my efforts to live with intention and gratitude, power and humility, focus and faith.

With no evidence of where I would work or what I would do, I marched boldly into ambiguity once again.

Life was changing rapidly for me. Divine alignment had placed me in a privileged position. Years of servitude and preparation gave birth to an opportunity weeks later to deliver the commencement speech at the same university to which my son had recently been accepted.

The significance of this ask did not go unnoticed. I would be responsible for sending a new cohort of innovators into the world while setting a precedent for how a predominately white institution of higher learning should view and receive my son.

In one day, I would fly to Los Angeles, deliver my most significant appeal at the University of Southern California's Iovine and Young Academy, and fly back home to send my son off to his senior prom.

I was living the Black American dream.

I was fully engaged in my family's healthy maturation, fully present and emotionally available for my children, and deeply in love with my exceptional other. I was the return on Barbara Jean Anderson's investment. I had become my ancestors 'wildest dreams and my progeny's future inspiration.

The lessons of our life define the shape and grandeur of our aspirations. Because my ancestors dared to endeavor to pursue a better life in the north during the Great Migration, I stood at the edge of opportunity, prepared to seize the day—a day I will never forget.

CHAPTER 20

THE REJECT AND THE REBEL

We know too much, and we feel too little.

Jerry and I kept in touch during my time in Chicago. We found a rhythm as friends that superseded our partnership with Adidas.

> *I think what you are doing is super important and destiny- and purpose-driven. I would hate to compromise that work to fit into a FOG perspective.*

He texted me this as we discussed the nature of my participation in the company as it advanced. I replied:

> *Looking forward to game planning when I am back. God's will is perfect and complete.*

When I returned from Chicago, I did not decide to leave Fear of God hastily. We had obsessed over every detail, strategic partner alignment, and resource allocation. Nothing was left to chance. Despite not having yet launched the product publicly, I knew my purpose resided beyond the walls of our headquarters.

Rather than man employing me, God was again deploying me.

My time was clearly coming to a close. My children's book, community-based speaking engagements, and desire to serve the youth dominated every conversation and every thought.

In times of transition, most people assume conflict is necessary to protect yourself against false assumptions of your intentions. Leaving a role, eliminating a position, or changing the function of a position comes with tension; however, I did not want this to be the case. I live by a code of honor and gratitude: principle and maturity.

There would be no big confrontation, only sound discussions and clear communication with our teams and partners. I wanted to show Black men could work together, resolve differences healthily, and end professional relationships gracefully. Our dedication to a higher power compelled us to have challenging discussions with sound minds and clear hearts.

I would remain a part of the FOG team for the next few months, methodically transferring my work, responsibilities, and strategy frameworks to the core leadership team. My main priority was leaving with integrity while striving to set my colleagues up for success.

Life continued to accelerate for us as our daughter was accepted into a magnificent art-and-design-focused high school in Southern California. We allowed our children to choose their best educational environment during their high school years. This act of stewardship gave them the confidence and self-efficacy to make sound choices and clearly understand the opportunity cost of adulthood.

The harsh reality of how society objectifies the Black body and productizes Black culture—often to our detriment—prompted us to give our children the tools of discernment and self-advocacy. The "adultification" of young Black girls compared to white girls of the same age leads to Black girls being perceived as needing less nurturing, comfort, and protection (Graham 2017).

The sooner our children learned how to command respect, navigate society, and deal with adults in positions of authority, the better prepared they would be to thrive in the face of these false assumptions of their maturity. Whether we like it or not, Black parents must give their sons and daughters "the talk" as they evolve from young children to young adults. No success nor education could shield our children from the reality of being young, gifted, and Black in America.

We prepared our daughter for high school while preparing our son for life as a college student. In two weeks, we had our son's prom, two graduations, my USC commencement speech, and a pending move. Layers of transitions were thrust upon us in one moment. The stress of so much change would usually cause friction and emotional toil.

However, our hearts knew we were being planted in fertile soil. The seeds we planted along our journey were beginning to bear fruit.

USC was the first of many harvests.

May 13, 2022, the moment I had been tirelessly preparing for, had finally arrived.

“Babe, wake up,” I said. “I am about to leave for the airport. Today is the day. Can you believe our son is going to prom today *and* I am giving a speech at USC? He’s going there next year. God is so good!” I rushed to finish getting dressed.

“God is so good, honey. I am proud of you,” Sonny replied as she prepared for the day. She would get our daughter to school while our son remained home, preparing for prom. He had his suit and flowers for the girls who would join him and his friends in their chartered sprinter van, and I had my speech. Finally, we were all ready for the emotional experience of seeing our eldest child attend one last dance before he departed on his adventure.

We held hands in a circle before going our separate ways. “God, thank you for the opportunity to be a blessing to my son and my family. Thank you for allowing me to speak life over the students at USC today. Lord, guide and protect everyone today as they prepare for prom and to receive their diplomas. Give my family traveling grace and mercy, Lord,” I prayed.

I rushed to San Jose Airport, parked my vehicle, and departed on time. Everything was in divine order.

My sister would attend the USC ceremony alongside my close friend, Gavin “Mizzle” Matthieu. He and I met during our trip to Israel and immediately formed a bond. He had a company called SuperVSN, and I had a company entitled Super Heroic. Our mothers favored one another, and he and I looked like we could be siblings. His family were proud residents of south-central Los Angeles, the place where I would deliver my commencement speech.

We all arrived on time, and Gavin sat front row while Tiarre and I sat quietly backstage, awaiting the arrival of the school's namesakes, world-renowned music executives Jimmy Iovine and Andre "Dr. Dre" Young.

"T, take a picture? I want to make sure I look fly," I asked discreetly to calm my nerves before giving the speech.

"Got you, Jace," she replied. I handed her my iPhone to capture the moment. Secretly, I wanted to review the photo to check out my beard, ensure my bald head was not too shiny, and ensure my outfit was indeed "swaggy."

After a few rounds of posing, my sister and I concluded I was indeed swagged out, and God was orchestrating the day.

"You ready? How are you feeling?" asked Lynn Miles, the associate dean of USC IYA, as we awaited the arrival of the school's esteemed founders.

"Okay, Jimmy and Dre have arrived," the producers' voices crackled over the walkie-talkies as we walked toward the closed curtain while the auditorium filled with eager students and emotionally engaged family members.

"Great to meet you both. My son is attending IYA this coming fall, so I guess we are family now," I said as Jimmy, Dre, and I were escorted from behind the curtain onto the stage.

"Man, that's wonderful news, brother. Wonderful news," Dre replied as we took our seats facing the crowd.

Jimmy leaned over and said, "You're going to kill it." Then he greeted the faculty and staff of IYA.

His support was the final encouragement I needed before taking the stage. After a few minutes of salutations and student reflections, Dean Rikkas welcomed me.

I arose, sweat dripping from my brow, walked gracefully to the podium, and delivered the remarks below, entitled, "The Reject and the Rebel."

2022 USC Iovine and Young Commencement Speech: "The Reject and the Rebel" by Jason Mayden

> I come to you today with a grateful heart.
>
> I am grateful for the opportunity to immerse myself in the beauty and preciousness of now.
>
> I am grateful for the overwhelming feeling of the profound love and adoration I hold within me for my beloved family. With their permission and support, I am here with you today.
>
> I am grateful for the revelation of serendipity that has placed me here as your keynote speaker while simultaneously rejoicing in the acceptance of my son, who will attend IYA in the fall.
>
> The majesty and mystery of purpose have unfolded in my life in ways that exist beyond words.

I am a child of the south side of Chicago.

I am the culmination of my ancestors 'sacrifices and the progenitor of my descendants 'well-doing.

I am all of us. Oklama (shout-out to Kendrick Lamar).

Today is an extremely momentous day for all of us. Collectively, we stand at the edge of eternity, full of might, invigoration, and a deep yearning to display our abilities.

I'd like to thank the faculty and administration of the Iovine and Young Academy for allowing me to share with you today.

I'd like to acknowledge and honor the parents, family members, and supporters of these tremendously talented and distinguished disruptors we are here to honor today.

Lastly, I would like to thank the students. Because of you, I am reminded of my journey.

Over the course of my career, I have realized two types of people exist within the social contract of reality we have agreed to. The way of life can be free and overwhelmingly beautiful, but we have lost the way, creating what some believe is a binary reality that exists at the intersection of . . . *the reject and the rebel.*

They are both common archetypes that have existed since the dawn of mankind.

They have wrestled for control of humanity's boldest endeavors throughout antiquity and into modern times.

In the most subtle way, they exist within us all in the forms of fear and doubt, joy and empathy.

However, the realities we have all individually agreed to have compelled us to choose a way, one of honor and gratitude, the other of greed, which has corrupted mankind's desire to pursue happiness and barricaded the world with hatred and dismay.

The way of the reject . . . is the refusal of truth.

Governance by fear and subjugation.

The reject believes the world does not exist beyond their perspective. They have become tethered to the myopic ethos that does not contribute to the tapestry of humanity's inner desire to create beauty.

Ego, venomous rhetoric, and toxic productivity fuel them.

They lack impeccability with their words, and they call upon the spirit of death to discourage the dreams of others, toiling all of their days to create a world in which they themselves cannot find peace.

They reject the natural ways of mankind.

The way of the rebel . . . is to despise the lies of men.

They are divinely compelled to break free from the tyranny of greed.

They create life and abundance through affirming words that bring forth a bounty of imagination and wonder.

Through introspection and self-awareness, they learn to lead.

They have accepted that their greatest enemy is their "inner me."

Fueled by compassion, they see themselves as being "deployed" by providence rather than "employed" by man.

They are owners of nothing but stewards of everything.

They fight for the preservation of man's natural desire to achieve true happiness.

The battle between the reject and the rebel has produced technology that has given us an abundance of efficiency but has left us in need of deeper connections to the world around us.

Misguided intellectual pursuits have distracted us from our sovereignty and worthiness.

We simply know too much, and we feel too little.

(Tone shift: call to action.)

It is incumbent upon you, the warriors of the light, to rise and create a decent new world free of greed, hatred, and the rejection of critical discourse and science.

The power of creation has been abused.

Natural resources have been privatized and distributed among the fortunate few.

You have the power to make this life free and beautiful.

You have the power to make this life a wonderful adventure through curiosity and intention.

It is no longer about what you can gain but rather what you can give.

Cleverness has made us cold and unkind.

Creativity dismantles the spiritual bondage of cynicism and deceit.

In Latin, the phrase *creatio ex nihilo* means "to create from nothing."

In a world where anything is possible, nothing is beyond your reach.

To achieve the impossible requires divergent thinking . . . radical faith in your truth. The real you. The one yearning to be seen but held captive by others' expectations.

Break free, warriors of the light!

The willingness to stand in the face of brutes and declare your truth is catalyzed by what you have learned over the course of your unlearning.

You have unlearned the ways of the world that have led many men to abandon their dreams because of a lack of courage.

You have unlearned the ways of a system designed to extract value from your purpose, leaving you to feel unloved and unworthy of all this beautiful world has to offer.

You have unlearned the ways of the reject and have moved toward the ways of the rebel.

Continue to move forward boldly!

Rely on your urgent desire to create what comes from nothing.

Use your imagination to build a new reality where your truth does not need to be explained.

You are mighty.

You are magnificent.

You are enough.

The fight for our collective well-being forges on.

The reject fights against . . . equality, justice, truth.

The rebel fights for . . . peace, love, harmony.

But you, magnificent, mighty warriors of the light, you are neither rejects nor rebels. You are Trojans.

For victory is ours, and we must fight until the world accepts that every man, woman, and child is created equal in the eyes of divine intelligence.

By creativity and compassion, I urge you to take action and live a life worthy of praise.

Fight for progress.

Fight for the preservation of humanity.

Fight for the dreams and aspirations of generations to come.

Fight on!

At the conclusion of the speech, I received a standing ovation.

I had "killed it," as Jimmy prophesied.

For the remainder of the ceremony, all eyes lay squarely on me. Every student who walked past me to receive their diploma nodded to support my remarks. I knew in my heart I had impacted Jimmy and Dr. Dre and an entire institution. I wanted to ensure my son would be welcomed into this environment and viewed in the proper light. I was earnestly working to capture respect and deliver inspiration.

I was fully prepared for my moment.

Time accelerated, and I could no longer linger in Southern California. In less than two hours, my flight back to San Jose would depart from Burbank, and I would rush to Oakland to be present for my son's prom. In fourteen hours, I had done what my seven-year-old self would consider impossible.

I inspired a new generation of innovators, met an influential figure from my childhood, created a wonderful moment with my sibling, and forged a deeper bond with my friend before rushing home to be present for my son's moment.

In my eyes, I shattered every stereotype about the Black male. I represented intelligence, confidence, grace, commitment, humility, compassion, love, and, of course, authentic swagger.

I had gone from the south side of Chicago to south-central LA to the south bay of San Francisco. Catalyzed by love and faith, we ended our chapter in the Bay Area in a grand fashion, one family unified under the guidance of divine provocation and deep commitment to our collective bond.

Now the Maydens would begin a new chapter, this time in Southern California.

Serendipity had once again found its way into our lives.

CHAPTER 21

HOMECOMING

September 16, 2022. Detroit, Michigan.

During our time at Nike as Black designers, D'Wayne Edwards, Jeff Henderson, E. Scott Morris, Wilson Smith, and I often met and discussed how we would scale access and opportunity to the communities we loved and adored. D'Wayne centered his efforts on skill development and exposure via a Nike-and-Jordan-Brand-led competition called Future Sole, which focused on providing pathways for young talent to enter the footwear design industry.

Future Sole would evolve into Pensole Academy in 2011, where D'Wayne continued to provide access, training, and opportunities to the next generation through his in-person training center, headquartered in downtown Portland, Oregon.

Jeff Henderson focused on understanding manufacturing and trade relations between North America and Asia. This interest allowed him to open Nike's first design pod in Tokyo, Japan, in 2006, where Jeff lived and worked with his family for over three years. While in Tokyo, he formed his thesis to successfully spark a revolution in domestic production in the US Midwest.

Wilson and E. Scott maintained a strong relationship inside corporate America. They thrived professionally at the intersection of team management and mentorship. They endeavored to be phenomenal leaders who provided guidance, support, care, and acknowledgment for a long lineage of diverse footwear designers who were encouraged to care deeply about servitude and community.

My path was a bit different.

I focused solely on value creation and how we could leverage creativity across multiple industries and sectors. I wanted to understand how businesses were initialized, funded, and scaled. The desire to protect and adequately reward Black and Brown intellectual property led me to Stanford's Graduate School of Business in 2010, where I would learn the mechanics of new venture creation.

We were deliberately aligned from the beginning. We set out to create pathways for our people and, in turn, created pathways for one another.

Our reunion in Detroit for the Black Footwear Forum served as the final stage in our twenty-year adventure. We were there to celebrate the opening of the first historically Black college focused on design in the United States, Pensole Lewis College of Business and Design.

Our skills and individual paths finally merged into one focused goal: providing culturally relevant training, professional development, and opportunities to Black and Brown designers.

While I prepared to travel back to Detroit for the first time since 2019, a wave of emotions overtook me.

"Babe, it's crazy I was the only Black kid that wanted to design shoes when I first got to CCS. Now we are heading back to open an entire school for Black kids in the place where I got my start. I began my journey alone. Now I am coming back with an army. God is grand," I said daily as our trip to Detroit approached.

"It's all God, babe. You pour your heart into mentoring and providing opportunities for people. Regardless of what they look like or where they come from. That's who you are. I hope you get everything you need from Detroit." Her words reminded me of my constant desire to be a servant leader for diverse creative youth.

The entire world had witnessed the murder of George Floyd 845 days before that moment. America's fragile brand of equality was dismantled and replaced with performative marketing campaigns positioned as a show of support for the Black community.

Over those 845 days, Black professionals in every industry endeavored to speak openly and boldly about the need for change. As a result, our plight complemented the unified agendas and purpose-built vocational communities.

Design as an industry was no different. Historically, the athletic footwear and apparel industry relied heavily on the cultural nuance, athletic ability, and tone of voice of the Black community to create products, services, and experiences that focused on converting our style, slang, and disposition into a commodity.

My career began as a student at the predominantly white institution of College for Creative Studies in Detroit, Michigan.

So naturally, I know and understand the nature of cultural appropriation as a design strategy.

For much of my academic and professional career, I was often the only person who looked like me in every room I entered. While I was at CCS, students who had come to Detroit with dreams of breaking into the automotive industry criticized my desire to design footwear.

The memory of being the only student who wanted to pursue a path considered peculiar and lowbrow at the time stayed with me throughout my career.

When D'Wayne Edwards first notified me we would hold the second annual Black Footwear Forum in Detroit, I immediately asked, "What do you need from me?"

He responded, "Lil bro, I need you to show up and do what you do. Talk to the people. Let them hear your voice. It's our time."

The BFF is a platform for Black professionals and allies from the footwear industry to convene, discuss the state of our profession, and celebrate the lives and careers of industry pioneers.

His ask was simple and direct. I needed to return to the place where my career began, a place that once stood as a symbol of my defiance now became a catalyst for change.

Upon our arrival, we noticed the expansive renovations at Detroit's Wayne County Airport. The signs of a rapidly changing metropolis lined the halls of DTW. Detroit felt foreign and familiar to Sonny and me.

"This place is completely different. Wow. This is crazy," I commented as we walked toward the rental car center.

Commercial interest replaced Detroit's gritty atmosphere to increase tourism and attract new industries to its once-booming downtown.

Dan Gilbert, a Detroit native, the cofounder of Rocket Mortgage and Rocket Ventures, and the owner of the Cleveland Cavaliers, had invested time and tremendous resources into his beloved hometown's revitalization.

Pensole Lewis was a direct benefactor of his generosity, investment, and influence. Having anchored the investment to acquire the property used for Pensole Lewis, he guaranteed the vision and purpose of the institution could serve students for generations to come.

The landscape of the community and its limited opportunities to advance have dramatically changed over the last ten years.

Once a wasteland of vacant high-rise buildings, abandoned factories, and dilapidated public transit facilities, Detroit's downtown had become home to some of the Midwest's best entertainment, sports, and hospitality facilities. Detroit's radiant culture was no longer a secret. The whole industry was descending on Detroit.

Its time had finally arrived.

Vibrant, diverse industries emerged, and a new vanguard of creative minds led the way.

The morning of our first day in Detroit, Sonny and I arranged a visit to CCS, where an eager group of industrial design students, faculty, and alumni waited for us. Weeks prior, I contacted Stephen Schock, the professor who supported my dream. I had made it a tradition to speak to his class whenever I visited, and this time would be no different.

"Good morning; thank you for taking the time to see me on your busy Friday. I appreciate your time." My opening remarks allowed me to center the room and assess the crowd's energy. During economic uncertainty and world division, I needed to bring hope and inspiration—a call to action for the creative youth. "We are standing at the edge of a creative revolution. A moment in time that will be defined not by what we do but rather what we refuse to do." My message was clear and concise. Their gifts and talents were essential to the society's advancement.

Creativity was their greatest weapon in the battle for equality.

They sat anchored to every word for more than an hour. Finally, we concluded by exchanging information and documenting the special moment with a group photo.

My heart was whole and my body was tired, but my mind was alert.

We departed CCS shortly after, heading toward a school full of elementary-school-age children eagerly waiting to meet me, D'Wayne, and Jeff. Three Black designers from various backgrounds conversed with Stephen Green, the COO of A Kids Company, the publisher of my first book, *A Kids Book about Design*.

Our early afternoon adventure formed the emotional foundation for the remainder of the trip with one part career panel and one part book signing.

The attentive faces of Black and Brown children engulfed in stories of creativity and wonder encouraged us all.

"It was so good to see you all. I really needed this. I really needed to see you all today." The words of a soft-spoken, handsome young Black boy melted the hearts of every adult gathered near the table where I sat and wrote personalized inscriptions for every child in attendance.

My time was their time. Each student was worthy of my attention, and I greeted them individually with affirmation and praise.

"It's a pleasure to meet you, young king. It's a pleasure to meet you, young queen." These were the words I spoke to every student as they approached the table to shake my hand and receive a copy of my book.

"I will never wash this hand again," several students said, symbolizing the importance of our presence. They viewed us as real-life superheroes, men who looked like them, doing things that were beyond their imagination.

We represented possible outcomes they had never once considered.

Our presence was the spark the minds of those gifted children needed to light the fire of creative passion.

We departed shortly after, returning to our hotel before gathering with the rest of the weekend attendees for a VIP reception at the downtown Detroit Pistons 'practice facility.

The evening was full of laughter and conversation.

The BFF had gathered multiple generations of Black footwear excellence in one room for one purpose: to honor and uplift our collective efforts.

Each conversation left me feeling progressively full of love and respect throughout the event.

"Man, I just want to give you your flowers. You represent us all so well. We love and appreciate you," I was told numerous times and in multiple ways by the event attendees.

D'Wayne wanted to create a homecoming for the footwear industry's Black and Brown contributors.

For me, it was more than a homecoming. It was a family reunion among former professors, mentors, mentees, and colleagues who all contributed to my complete acceptance of my journey and identity.

The next day, the educational programming would begin. The day would kick off with opening remarks from George Floyd's brother, who spoke of the importance of community and restitution. Each panel discussion touched on relevant aspects of our industry, our values, and our desired next steps as a community.

We were the ones we had been waiting for.

While transitioning from each activity, students, industry execs, and former colleagues approached and held me in deep conversation. They chose to speak life over me. They desired to make me feel valued and uplifted. The people I have always aspired to represent with honor and gratitude showered me with heartfelt praise.

Overcome with emotion, I frequently removed myself from those conversations to withdraw to the lecture hall where I would sit in silence, moved with a deep appreciation for the moment.

Having left Fear of God to pursue my purpose again, I felt unsure about what to expect from the homecoming. I feared everyone would want me to explain in great detail why I left my prestigious role alongside Jerry Lorenzo. But, to my surprise, everyone opted to shower me with love and appreciation instead. They had heard the rumors and collectively decided not to pry. Their plan was centered on love and upliftment, not gossip and clout chasing.

Ironically, I found the healing I needed in the place that once caused me so much pain. Detroit solidified my work ethic twenty years prior; now, it gave me creative rejuvenation.

Our journey back to California consisted of nonstop discussions of the transformative experience.

"Sonny, I feel like me again. I feel full."

"Oh honey, I'm so happy to hear that. You deserve to feel loved," she replied as we entered our home.

I carried the energy and support of an army of brilliant melanated minds. I was no longer alone, fighting for a place in the world.

I had found my passion once again in the place where it all began.

My life's pace led me to the origins of my modern reality. Letting go of the pain of the past, I harmoniously navigated the ambiguity of the months preceding our time in Detroit.

My career aspirations expanded while my love for my wife and children deepened. As a result, my life's trajectory shifted and fell in alignment with my divine intention to serve our youth.

We often try to control the outcome of every endeavor. We affiliate our self-worth with our resilience and trauma tolerance. No one should have to be so strong as a child. Unfortunately, this hardening of our emotions during our youth blocks us from feeling satisfied and deserving of our blessings.

By breaking free and honoring the inner call to adventure, I accepted the moment for what it was: the ending of my beginning and the beginning of my tomorrow.

Purpose and faith once again compelled me to choose the road less traveled.

God's plan gave me a new rhythm and a renewed focus.

I was finally moving at the speed of grace.

ACKNOWLEDGMENTS

To my family, friends, and colleagues, I offer a sincere word of thanks and gratitude for the countless lessons and examples you have provided to my life. I started this journey nervous and unsure how to tell my narrative concisely. I have been through so much, and many of you have witnessed my trials and triumphs. Therefore, I intentionally altered names, locations, and details to protect your identities and vulnerable memories.

I am honored and humbled you have all poured into me. Your stories, details, and feedback have proven invaluable to me, my ancestors, and my future progeny.

Mom, Dad, AC, Tiarre, Sodi, Shani, Niyah, Ace, Donnie, Sonny, Khalil, Viviana, and Coltrane, I love and appreciate you more than words can describe. You are my why. I hope I have made you all proud. I know over the years I have not always been kind to myself. My trauma caused me to reject love when I needed it the most. But you have never given up on me, and I will never give up on you either. As Grandma Bootsie told us before and after she passed, never lose faith. God can and will provide.

To my mentors and teachers, thank you for seeing me for who I am. I am grateful to have had Black women such as Mrs. Blackwell and Mrs. Caldwell as my teachers after experiencing the heartache that resulted from a culturally insensitive teacher a year prior.

I am grateful for Mr. Summers and his example of selfless, nonjudgmental love. I wish he was still alive to see who I became. I know he is smiling down from heaven. He was the first person to believe in my artistic abilities. I hope I have made him proud.

I am grateful for Professor Schock and his bold example of faith-driven love. First, he fought to make space for me and my aspirations at CCS. Then, years later, I realized he was a man of faith who saw in me something worth fighting for.

I am grateful to Dr. Aaker and Professor Flink. You came into my life during a period of personal crisis, and you never let me down. You have mentored my children, provided professional guidance, and, more importantly, have become some of my closest friends.

To my beta readers, editors, and crowdfunding supporters, writing this book was the hardest thing I have ever done creatively. The second hardest thing was allowing you all to see the messiness of this process. As a self-professed perfectionist, sharing raw, unedited stories full of spelling errors, grammatical mistakes, and uncited references was an act of faith. But I trusted if I showed up fully throughout this process, you would do the same. Your input, advice, and feedback have been more than I imagined.

Tiffany, Cheresse, Grant, Michael, Jonathan, Bridget, and Reggie, you are appreciated. Thank you for allowing me to borrow three weeks of your time. Your feedback, candor, and commitment to my success are recognized and well received.

I look forward to supporting you all along your journey as well.

Lastly, thank you, the reader, for choosing my book and taking the time to learn more about my story. I hope I can inspire you to take action, heal from your trauma, and live a life full of love, creativity, and self-acceptance.

With honor and gratitude,

Jason "JayMay" Mayden

1 Corinthians 16:14

APPENDIX

CHAPTER 1: THE FALLACY OF FEAR

Mann, Kiran. 2021. "Council Post: Brace Yourself for the Great Resignation: A Note to the Leaders." Forbes. November 1, 2021. Accessed September 29, 2022. https://www.forbes.com/sites/forbescoachescouncil/2021/11/01/brace-yourself-for-the-great-resignation-a-note-to-the-leaders.

Rudy, Lisa Jo. 2022. "The Neurodivergent Brain: Everything You Need to Know." Verywell Health. February 4, 2022. Accessed October 25, 2022. https://www.verywellhealth.com/neurodivergent-5216749.

CHAPTER 2: THE REAL-LIFE DR. LUCIUS FOX

Johns Hopkins Medicine. 2022. "Septicemia." The Johns Hopkins University. Accessed November 19, 2022.
https://www.hopkinsmedicine.org/health/conditions-and-diseases/septicemia.

CHAPTER 3: WALKING BAREFOOT THROUGH THE GRASS

Picker, Les. 2007. "Does Child Abuse Cause Crime?" National Bureau of Economic Research. January 2007. Accessed October 30, 2022. https://www.nber.org/digest/jan07/does-child-abuse-cause-crime.

CHAPTER 4: ONE HUNDRED AND EIGHTY SECONDS

Psychology. 2016. "Culture of Honor." *Psychology* (blog), IResearchNet. February 1, 2016.
https://psychology.iresearchnet.com/social-psychology/cultural-psychology/culture-of-honor/.

Illinois Policy. 2013. "Trapped in Chicago's Worst Schools: Education Outcomes in Chicago's Lowest-Performing Public Schools." Reports. October 24, 2013. Accessed July 18, 2022.
https://www.illinoispolicy.org/reports/trapped-in-chicagos-worst-schools-education-outcomes-in-chicagos-lowest-performing-public-schools/.

CHAPTER 8: THE BENCH

Hatfield, Tinker. 2014. "Sole Decade Top 10 Interviews // Tinker Hatfield on the Birth of Training." Interviewed by Nick DePaula and Zac Dubasik. Sole Collector. January 13, 2014. Accessed September 15, 2022. https://solecollector.com/news/2014/01/sole-decade-top-10-interviews-tinker-hatfield-on-the-birth-of-training.

CHAPTER 10: RISE OF THE JUMPMAN

Carr, Jesse. 2021. "Designer Spotlight: Wilson Smith III." SoleSavy. May 18, 2021. Accessed September 3, 2022. https://solesavy.com/designer-spotlight-wilson-smith-iii/.

CHAPTER 12: DELAYED DOES NOT MEAN DENIED

Lusk, Veneta. 2019. "The Market Crash of 2008 Explained." Wealthsimple. Last updated June 5, 2019. Accessed September 21, 2022. https://www.wealthsimple.com/en-ca/learn/2008-market-crash#about_the_2008_stock_market_crash.

Rogoway, Mike. 2009. "Nike Will Cut 1,750 Jobs, Including 500 at Oregon Headquarters." OregonLive—The Oregonian. May 15, 2009. Accessed August 14, 2022. https://www.oregonlive.com/business/2009/05/500_oregon_jobs_among_1750_nik_1.html.

CHAPTER 13: GASSED UP

Psychology Today Staff. 2022. "Imposter Syndrome." Psychology Today. Accessed September 22, 2022. https://www.psychologytoday.com/us/basics/imposter-syndrome.

CHAPTER 16: DESERT OF NEGEV

White, Rachel E., Emily O. Prager, Catherine Schaefer, Ethan Kross, Angela L. Duckworth, and Stephanie M. Carlson. 2016. "The 'Batman Effect': Improving Perseverance in Young Children." Child Development 88, no. 5 (December 16, 2016): 1563–1571. https://doi.org/10.1111/cdev.12695.

CHAPTER 20: THE REJECT AND THE REBEL

Graham, Ruth. 2017. "Black Girls Are Too Often Treated as Older Than They Are—and Suffer for It." Slate. June 28, 2017. Accessed September 25, 2022. https://slate.com/human-interest/2017/06/black-girls-are-seen-as-being-older-than-their-age.html.

CPSIA information can be obtained
at www.ICGtesting.com
Printed in the USA
BVHW050253270223
659263BV00007B/62